AF553362

Changing Profile of Financial Services

Changing Profile of Financial Services

Edited by

B. L. MATHUR

Discovery Publishing House
New Delhi-110002 (India)

Published by :

Discovery Publishing House
4831/24, Ansari Road,
Darya Ganj,
New Delhi – 110002
Phone– 3279245

FIRST PUBLISHED 1997

Reprinted-2011

ISBN 81-7141-398-6.

Typesetting :
PRIYANKA COMPUTERS
B.S. ROAD
JAIPUR 320 001

Printed at:
Mehra Offset Press
Delhi

Preface

Financial service institutions in India have made fascinating growth during last two decades by rendering various types of services as merchant bankers, issue and lead manager, mutual fund operator, off-shore and venture fund operator, portfolio manager, lease financer, housing-financer and bills-dis-counting houses. Under the new dispensation, the financial service sector faces new challenges. The liberalisation policies pursued by the Government of India have called for more competitiveness and efficiency in the financial service sector. The current expansion in financial services alongwith stock markets has been supported by structural transformation of the economy is, no doubt, a direct outcome of the liberalisation process.

The rising business and profits of the financial services companies against the backdrop of the disappointing performance of companies in the core sector as also the banking sector have attracted entrepreneurs to this segment witnessed a boom in investment.

In this view, an attempt is made in this book to venture into the areas of mutual funds, commercial paper, factoring, forfaiting, Development Banks, Venture Capital, OTCEI, Deposit Insurance & Credit Guarantee Corporation, Credit Risk Management and Lease Financing etc. The comprehensive book focuses on a wide range of issues concerning management of financial services in India. The book includes chapters authored by leading experts of the field from different parts of the country.

I take this opportunity of expressing my deep sense of gratitude to all the contributors who despite their preoccupation have responded generously to my request, without their response, it would not have been possible for me to bring out the book in its present shape. The support and co-operation of all the contributors have been a great source of strength and encouragement for me. My acknowledgments are also due to the *PNB Monthly Review* for reproduce chapter fifth and eleventh and to *Bank of India Bulletin* for reproduce chapter tenth and twelfth in this volume.

This volume has been prepared under the auspices of the *Institute of Management Science*, Jaipur.

It is hoped that the volume would be welcomed by the academic community and found useful by researchers, policy makers, financial services managers and institution builders concerned with working and performance of financial services.

To Discovery Publishing House New Delhi. I acknowledge my thanks for bringing out the publication in a record time. I am solely responsible for any omission and inconsistencies in the book and look forward for constructive suggestions from readers.

B. L. Mathur

The Contributors

1. *Nalini Prava Tripathy*
Faculty Member
Regional College of Management
BHUBANESWAR

2. *Mohd. Akbar Ali Khan*
Reader
Department of Commerce
Aligarh Muslim University
ALIGARH.

3. *Bhibhuti B. Pradhan*
Reader & Head
Department of Commerce
University of Imphal
MANIPUR.

4. *Dr. K. Satyanarayana*
Chief
Long Range Planning &
Innovative Banking Division
Punjab National Bank
NEW DELHI.

5. *Dr. Rita Mathur*
Faculty Member
Department of Economic Administration
and Financial Management
University of Rajasthan.
JAIPUR.

6. *Dr. Mayura Pandya*
Chief Officer
Bank of India
BOMBAY

7. *T. N. K. Iyer*
Chief Officer
Management Information
Service Department
Bank of India
BOMBAY

8. *K. Ram Mohan*
Senior Manager
Head Office
Punjab National Bank
NEW DELHI.

9. *Dr. B. L. Mathur*
Faculty Member
Department of Economic Administration
and Financial Management
University of Rajasthan.
JAIPUR.

10. *Dr. Rajive Saxena*
Faculty Member
Department of Economic Administration
and Financial Management
University of Rajasthan.
JAIPUR.

Contents

1

Commercial Paper Market – The Changing Scenario

Nalini Prava Tripathy

The four and half decades of the Indian freedom has led the country through a divergent face of development. This paper throws light on the recent development of the commercial paper market, challenges and opportunities in the coming years".

There has been a tremendous growth in the Indian capital market during the eighties along with process of liberalisation and is passing through a phase of structural transformation. The number of players have been increased and several new instruments have been launched in money market. In this context, disintermediation is one of the most important development in the Indian financial market. the concept come from the realization that due to cross subsidisation of lending rates and high reserve requirements, the company seldom requires the intermediation of the bank for the mobilisation of resources. So commercial paper has come into practice to give an opportunity to well-rated companies as an alternative changes to raise short term funds directly from the market.

Commercial paper is traceable in the early nineteenth century and was developed only in the second decade of the 20th century. The 'Chakravarty Committee' and subsequently the 'Vaghul working groups on money market' set up by the Reserve Bank, submitted its report in January 1987, recommended for the introduction of commercial paper in India. The introduction of commercial paper in the Indian financial market from January 1, 1990 has been one of the important policy initiatives of the RBI towards disintermediation process.

Conceptual Issues

Commercial paper is a short-term unsecured instrument issued by a company in the form of promissory notes with fixed maturities. The maturity period ranges from three months to less than 1 year. Since it is a short-term debt, the issuing company is required to meet dealers fees, rating agency fees, and any other relevant charges. CP has gained its popularity in all over the world because they provide funds relatively at a lower cost. Another important feature of CP is that through this instrument the firm may raise large amount of funds which is not possible from a single bank.

Eligibility for Issues of Commercial Paper

In India, the emergence of CP has added a new dimension to the money market. Hence, the RBI relaxed the initial guidelines which was laid down for the issue of CPs. The following are the guidelines governing commercial paper.

1. The CP has to be issued at discount in the forms of promissory note where interest is always front-ended and maturity values is always equal to face value.

2. As issuing firm must have a networth of atleast Rs. 4 crores and the company should have fund based working capital limit of Rs. 4 crores.

3. The current ratio should be 1.33:1 and debt-equity ratio not more than 1.5:1.

4. It must have a credit rating of P2/A2 or higher from the CRISIL/ICRA of not less than two months old at the time of issue of C.P. But this condition has become optional in the latter part of 1994.

5. The RBI has made mandatory for banks, consortia and syndicates to restrict the cash credit component to 75 percent of the maximum permissible bank finance and the overall capacity of each borrower to issue CPs is 56 percent of a borrower's maximum permissible bank finance.

6. The company must be listed on one or more stock exchanges. But the Government companies are exempt from this stipulation.

7. The issue of CP also bears the expenses of stamp duty and required to obtain the approval of the Reserve Bank for each issue of commercial paper.

8. Now the RBI abolished the facility of stand by arrangement as a result it is no longer mandatory for banks to automatically restore the cash credit limits of corporate bodies.

9. CP can be issued to any person or corporate bodies registered or incorporated in India (including banks) as well as non-incorporated bodies.

10. The issuing company is required to appoint a bank or leader of the consortium bank to verify the signature of the issuing company who have signed on the CP.

11. The issuing company is required to appoint a dealer who would arrange the investor for the commercial paper.

12. CP is generally issued at a discount and freely transferable by endorsement and delivery is not subject to tax deducted at source.

13. The face value of a single commercial paper should not be less than in 25 lakh and in multiples of Rs. 5 lakh thereafter.

Advantage of Commercial Paper

The advantage of CPs lies in its implicity as large amounts can be raised without having any underlying transaction. Secondly, it provides flexibility to the company to raise funds in the money market where it is favourable. Thirdly CP raises fund from the inter-corporate market which is not under the control of monetary authority. Fourthly CPs provides cheaper finance to the borrowers and at the same time also provides good rate of return to the investors.

Growth of CP Market

The CP market is a nascent stage and is facing number of practical difficulties. No doubt it is a low cost source of financing but it has not gained much popularity from the investors rather banks are invested in CP due to hassles. During 1990-91, out of the 29 companies which issued CPs. 8 were able to raise funds at 12 percent or less, 13 companies were able to raise funds between 12 and 14 percent and the remaining companies raised funds between 14 and 15 percent. The issue express in minority of cases were nil or less than one percent. From 1990 to march 1993 CPs issued in our country aggregated to Rs. 27 billion. During 1992-93, 44 companies were issued 125 CPs for an aggregate amount of Rs. 1438 crores and nearly 93 percent of issues were in the PI + AI + category of credit rating and the remaining were in PI/AI. The discount rate varied from 15 to 21 percent. About 81 percent of these issues were for a maturity period of three months. There are some signs of revival of CP market since early 1992 and the growth of CPs in Indian financial market increased in a very short duration of time. It has gained popularity due to strict measures taken by Government on the economic policy after the banking scam which led to the lendable surplus with the banking system and paucity of investment opportunities for short-term surplus. Therefore now the cash-rich companies including the oil companies are issuing commercial paper. The growth of CPs outstanding upto end of March 1993 is as follows

Commercial Paper Outstanding

Amount outstanding (Rs. in Crores)

	March	June	September	December
1990	85.50	156.40	193.70	178.10
1991	100.10	93.10	90.90	134.30
1992	332.65	198.05	317.05	733.05
1993	577.25	–	–	–

The Model

Keeping the amount outstanding (Rs. in crores) of CPs market in India, the growth of CPs market since March 1993 are predicted quarterly basis taking into account March 1991 as base year. To predict the commercial papers outstanding since March 1993, Least square technique has been employed and it has been assumed that there has been a linear growth of commercial paper outstanding in the Indian industrial sector as has been evidence from the above date i.e., in march 1991, the CPs outstanding was Rs. 85.50 crores whereas with a span of two years in March 1993, the CPs outstanding have grown upto Rs. 577.25 crores. Therefore the least square technique y = a +bx where 'X' is independent variable relating to the time period under study and 'Y' is dependent variable in Rs. to be predicted in future, 'a' is a constant in the slope representing 'Y' and 'b' is the slope representing the ratio of (y-a) that bears to 'x'. Hence by taking the summation of both sides and again multiplying both sides by 'x' we get the two normal equation as :

$$\Sigma y - a + bx \qquad (1)$$

$$\Sigma xy = a\Sigma x + b\Sigma x^2 \qquad (2)$$

Putting the respective value in the above two equation we get

3190.15 = 13a and 6893.3 = 182b

and hence a = 245.396 and b = 37.875 computing and putting the above results in the equation y = 1 + bx, the prediction for various future periods can be calculated as :

	March	June	September	December
1993	577.25	510.421	548.396	586.271
1994	624.146	662.021	699.896	737.771
1995	775.646	813.521	851.396	889.271
1996	927.146	965.021	1002.893	1040.771

Concluding Observations

The present study has pointed out a few important aspects of the problems and prospects of CPs in Indian money market. The introduction of the CP in the Indian money market has been welcomed but so far the total amount of CPs issue has net been spectacular. Even if the credit rating agencies are having proposals of CP issues but it is witnessing an unpopular phase due to the recent guidelines by the RBI in last October to abolish the facility of stand by arrangement under which banks are not mandatory to automatically restore the cash credit limits of corporate sectors and if the issuer needs a higher cash credit limit after being issued CPs, it would have to approach banks to increase the limit. Further the banks are shy away from the CP market as there is no guarantee of corporates returning to the original bank, once the CP matures. Another reason for downfall of CPs is the prevailing high call money rate. Even though the borrowers are interested to raise CPs, but there are no banks to finance them. Therefore the future growth and the character of the CP market in India will be dependent on the scope for innovation and support and regulatory framework provided by the monetary authorities. Another area which need to be strengthen by the monetary authority to increase the resources available with the DFHI to make the secondary market effective and provide liquidity investors.

No doubt, the prospects of CP market in India are extremely bright but the RBI should remove mandatory and time – consuming requirement of credit rating and to protect the interests of the investor, the standby facility could be mandatory for which a fee should be prescribed and stamp duty should be eliminated. In keeping with the reform process, some of the guidelines should be relaxed so as to broad-base the CP market. Considering the trend, the CP market have a vast potential in India to emerge as one of the important segments of the money market in future.

Reference

1. Goyal, M., "Commercial Paper Market : Its Development in Indian Context". *The Journal of the Indian Institute of Bankers,* April-June 1991.
2. Kurup, N. P., "Commercial Paper market : Scope in the Indian context" *P. N. B. Monthly Review,* March 1990.
3. Ohja, J., "Commercial Paper : Its Development in the Indian Context" *State Bank of India Monthly Review,* June, 1991.
4. Ramola, K. S. and Negi, K. S., "In Production of Commercial Paper (CPs) in Indian Finance Market : Implications and Developments" *Indian Banking Today and Tomorrow,* May, 1992.
5. Aagol, M., "Commercial Paper Market in Indian Growth and Prospects" *The Indian Journals of Commerce,* Vol. No. XLX Part–II, June, 1992.
6. Kamath, S. R., "Commercial Paper Market in India", *Chartered Secretary,* July, 1993.

7. Agrawal, Sanjiv, "The Indian Money market" Facts for you January, 1994.

8. Kumar Rakesh, "Commercial Paper : Gaining popularity" *The Chartered Accountant,* August, 1994.

9. *The Economic Times,* April 1995.

10. Tripathy, Nalini Prava " Commercial Paper in Indian Financial Market" *Indian Banking by 2000 A.D.*, Kaniska Publishers, Delhi, 1995.

Appendix – 1

The Working Group on the Money Market Headed by Mr. N. Vaghul (the Vaghul Committee), has set out the Following Framework for Developing the CP Market.

1. The CPs would be unsecured promissory notes (not tied to any specific transaction) sold directly by issuers to investors (excluding NRIs) or placed with investors through the agency of banks or other financial agencies.

2. The issuing company's net worth should be not less than Rs. 5 crores and its shares must be listed on the stock exchange and the company must be a party subject to the CAS. (However, subsequent to the *VC's recommendation,* the RBI has abolished the CAS).

3. The issuing company must get a credit rating from a recognised Credit Rating Agency, once every six months. Companies with only a minimum of "A" rating would be permitted to enter the CP market.

4. The maturity could be 15 days and over, but not exceeding 6 months with, if necessary, a Revolving Underwriting Facility of less than three years.

5. The minimum denomination of CPB could be Rs. 5 lakhs and the minimum amount of issue by a company could be Rs. 1 crore.

6. The interest rate on CP could be market determined and the paper could be issued at a discount to face value or it could be interest bearing.

7. The RBI would authorise the programme size of a company and the timing of issues to ensure an orderly queue.

   The authorisation would be issued both to the bankers of the company and the company and when the issue is actually placed on the market, it will be the responsibility of the concerned banks to reduce the permissible working capital limits to the extent of the issue under advise of the RBI.

8. The issuers would be required to meet dealers' fees, rating, agency fees and other charges including charges for stand-by facilities with banks and these should together not exceed a total of 1% of the amount raised.

9. The Finance House would impart liquidity to the CP by quoting two-way prices in the secondary market.

10. The instrument should not be subject to stamp duty at the time of issue and there should not be any tax deduction at source.

11. The CP should be freely transferable by endorsement and delivery and there should be no stamp fees on such transfers.

12. Legislative amendments or necessary exemptions would be required to ensure that various legal provisions do not inhibit the active development of the CP market.

2

Mutual Funds to Boost Capital Market - Indian Experience

Mohd. Akbar Ali Khan

Introduction

One of the long term measures invariably suggested to boost the present capital market is the setting up of Mutual Funds to encourage investors with substantial liquidity to enter the share market. The experience of some of the advanced countries, especially the US, has been very encouraging and within a short period of time excellent results have been achieved in mobilising resources for faster economic growth and investors are being given the widest ever opportunity to invest their funds to best serve their purpose. Statistics revealed that mutual funds has witnessed phenomenal growth in many countries during the last five years ranging from 80 percent of the total investments in USA to 70 per cent in Italy, 60 per cent in Japan and 50 per cent in UK are institutionalized in mutual funds. In US, there were 1531 mutual funds, with 30 million fund investors and $ 252 billion in assets at the end of 1986.

The objectives of this paper are two fold :

1. to attempt to study various advantages of mutual funds as a financial service to boost the capital market; and

2. to study its suitability for investors in Indian financial environment.

What is Mutual Fund ?

Definitions

1. "Mutual fund is a non-depository non-banking financial Intermediary"

2. "Mutual funds are corporations which pool funds and reduce risk by diversification".

Mutual Fund is a professionally managed company that combines the money of people whose goals are similar. It invests this money in a wide variety of securities. There are different kinds of mutual funds to serve the needs of different investors with diverse objectives. A mutual fund pools the savings of the community and invest them after careful research and analysis, in various types of securities and offers the individual saver advantages of reasonably dividends and capital appreciation, coupled with safety and liquidity. Basically, the mutual fund is similar, in structure and objective, to an investment club. The investor instead of making direct purchase of shares and bonds through original subscription or stock exchanges and take the risk of loss, can do so now through mutual funds.

The Concept of Mutual Fund

The concept of mutual funds originated in the 19th century in the UK and the US with the formation of large investment trusts during that period. In 1873, Robert Fleming formed the Scottish Americal Investment Trust. Trust's portfolio consisted solely of bonds floated by Amercial rail-road companies. In today's terminology there are two types of mutual funds :

– *The Open-Ended*, in which the investment company itself issues and redeems shares to and from the public every day. The example of open end mutual funds are units of Unit Trust of India and Can Stock of Canbank.

– *The Closed-ended fund,* which issues definite number of shares to the public only once. Any subsequent purchase or sale must be made through an 'over-the-counter' dealer or an exchange specialist. The example of closed and mutual funds are Master share issued by Unit Trust of India and Can share issued by Canbank fund.

A good deal of the popularity of Mutual fund can be attributed to the growing sense of futility among many investors over their inability to select individual securities in a volatile, complex market place. The small investors are able to have access to the big leagues of investing, and the cash management functions are simplified even for professional and institutional investor. Advantages of mutual funds as a vehicle for investment in capital market securities are manifold. Some of them as follows:

1. An Indepth Coverage of the Entire Spectrum of Investment

Till recent past we had to deal only with a handful of stocks and bonds, which were rather simple straight forward investments. Today, the situation is not exactly the same. Rather it is much more complex. Mutual funds have unique ability to overcome the difficulties created by complexity. There are individuals who continue to feel capable of selecting individual securities some via brokerage house research reports; others via intensive reading of financial journals, yet others by tips and recommendations from friends and associates. But for those who are not comfortable with such methods, the necessary answer is mutual funds. Whatever be the objectives and ability to absorb risk, there could be a mutual fund to fit that. A full range of investment alternatives can be build into an investment portfolio at a minimum of effort in today's hectic lifestyle of an individual because of the efficiency provided by the funds. There is no need to spend hours of precious time looking over publications and research reports and then relying on some else's judgement.

2. Reporting of Investment Results

There are no rules which govern the reporting of results by private investment managers. This is not true of mutual funds, especially open-ended funds. Since open-ended funds must also compute a net asset value (NAV) every day. NAV is an irrefutable public record of the funds management performance history. With mutual funds what you see, what you get. In advanced countries like US, a umber of statistical services are available to investors which take the daily data and create long term performance records for the interested investors to study. Generally, the data are for various time periods and classify the funds according to their investment objectives. So, a reader can know information most pertinent to his particular situation. If, for instance, one is interested in his current income, one can examine the long term and short term performance records of funds to see whether they are classified as seeking income or primarily fixed income issued.

3. A Consistent Investment Philosophy

The investment goal sought by an investor may either be current income long term growth, or some combination of the two. However, there is no way to guarantee that the desired objective could best be achieved by investing in a particular type of security. If the portfolio manager feels that another objective is more prudent in clients may well end up with a portfolio quite unlike the one 'contracted for'. But this is not so with mutual funds. In its prospectus, each fund must clearly state its investment objective. However, there are some shortcomings regarding the clarity of prospectus language. But, to quote from the Investment Company Institute, USA :

> "Nothing is foolproof, but the fact is that as a result of the series of checks and balances built into the mutual fund operating structure by the Investment company Act, not a single case of disinvestment fund has developed since 1940 in USA".

4. Full-Time Professional Management

One of the root causes for the inability of the traditional stock and bond approach to succeed in the present market environment has been the lack of full time professional management. In fact, studies have shown that individuals responsible for managing the portfolio of clients spend up to 10 per cent of their time on the solicitation and servicing of clients. In other words, such individuals are concerned with marketing, as not managing.

On the other hand, mutual fund managers, as they are rarely made available for marketing purposes, can devote their full time in managing portfolios. The fund's main marketing tools are sales materials, the prospectus and in some cases a sales force directly dealing with the public. Mutual fund portfolio managers who are insulated from client solicitation and retention are in an ideal position to devote their full talents to their main purpose managing portfolios, not marketing.

5. Pressure – Free Decisions

The individual managers often fall victims to the pressures brought about by their clients. Even though such managers may be resolute about their investment decisions, their will power is subject to a break-down when they are questioned by the client who pay their fees for management. On the other hand, investor has no way to apply pressure directly on the portfolio manager of a Mutual fund or to question him as to why certain decisions are made. Even at the annual meeting, an investor can't raise issues like inclusion in the portfolio of a particular stock favourity to him with the portfolio manager. The portfolio managers of Mutual Funds are in an excellent promotion to make pressure-free decisions.

6. Daily Record of Performance

If the investments of an investor are managed by a bank, brokerage firm or independent investment counsellor, he will receive a monthly, quarterly, by-annual or annual statement describing the activity in the account since the last report, current investments and their total value. But in the fast moving market place of today such reporting is not really up-to-date. However, such is not the case with mutual fund. Though it might not be easy to know about day to day changes in the composition of one's portfolio, one may be able to ascertain the satisfactory performance of funds on a daily basis.

7. Savings of Management Changes

Mutual funds provide a significant savings to investors on the costs of the administration, operation and management of their portfolios. For instance, Mutual funds are very large purchasers of stocks and bonds and can negotiate for more favourable rates with broken. By being a part of this large pool of investment capital, small investors and institutions enjoy indirectly the benefit of much lower transactions costs.

Mutual Funds – Indian Experience

Mutual funds are ideally suited to Indian financial environment. The suitability for investors in India has been legitimised by the Union government by amending the Banking Regulations Act to provide for setting up of mutual funds by Banking Companies as a legal activity. The notification enables commercial banks to set up subsidiaries which could be members of the stock exchanges. The notification specified that mutual funds would engage in business of acquisition, holding, management, trading or disposal of securities, participation certificates or any other instrument. Mutual funds could also engage themselves in the generation of income or growth participation business as also involve in the different schemes of the Unit Trust. The funds will be open to participation by the members of the public through the subscription of shares or units or otherwise for the purpose of providing facilities for participation in or distribution of the income, profits or gains arising from these activities to the participating members.

The mutual fund are legally allowed to make investment in a wide variety of operations. It includes all types of shares, debentures, bonds of any company, corporate body, company deposits, deposits with other corporate bodies, scheduled banks and similar institutions, any commercial paper or securities floated by the central Government, State Government, the Reserve Bank of India or any local authority outside of India and approved by the Reserve Bank of India. Also, the Mutual Funds will be allowed to invest in government securities as defined in the public debt Act, 1944. Following are the main points in support of the applicability of Mutual Funds in India :

1. India, being a poor country has predominance of small investors who have the ability to save small amounts. In recent years, they are also willing to invest in shares and debentures, but hesitate to do so because of lack of market information, their inability to reach the market quickly, difficulties they faces, in transacting business and obtaining liquidity in the secondary market. In India, even regular investors, do not possess requisite expertise needed for security analysis and for selecting appropriate investment portfolios. A need for professionally managed mutual funds has grown in recent years as stock exchanges are becoming more volatile and complex.

2. The size of the investing population in Indian stock exchanges is quite large. It is the largest next, only to that of the USA and Japan. It is extremely difficult to arrange for direct individual participation on stock exchanges for investing population. Indirect participation through mutual funds is an ideal solution to this problem.

3. At present, more than 90 per cent of the total value of shares and debentures is held by urban population residing in industrially advanced, educationally forward and financially sophisticated western region of the country. The population of the rest of the urban and the entire rural and semi-urban regions has command over an enormous pool of savings. Yet, it is financially unsophisticated to deal directly with the stock exchanges. The stock exchange in their turn do

not have well developed administrative machinery to reach them. Under these circumstances, mutual funds could be the ideal financial intermediaries bringing investing population which is denied access to stock exchanges which are unable to reach them because of administrative inadequacies.

4. There has been a poor balance of trade situation and mounting deficits, it has increasingly become necessary to tap the savings of foreign investors (including non-resident Indians) through a number of mutual funds since foreign investors have no expert knowledge about Indian companies and rules and regulations governing investments in India for efficient management of their portfolios.

5. The various segments of the capital market, primary issue market, secondary markets in shares and debentures, markets for gilt-edged securities, even money markets could be developed and integrated into one financial market through operation of mutual funds which are active simultaneously on more than one market.

6. India, like USA is a counter of continental size with diversity of investing population. There is great need and scope for a large variety of mutual funds in India. The scope of mutual fund is so broad that it covers the entire spectrum of investment requirements of the investors both domestic and foreign.

The Unit Trust of India (UTI) has been the country's first financial institution to have successfully launched various mutual fund schemes mainly because of the unique tax advantage it enjoys. Similar tax advantage will be made available to mutual funds started by nationalised banks and the amendment to the companies Act regarding this, is expected to be introduced in the parliament very soon. Thus, the income from such mutual funds will be tax-free in the hands of holders and no tax will be deducted at source while distributing income, under section 80C and 80L of the Indian Income Tax Act 1961.

Taking the advantage of the liberalised policy and obtaining necessary approval from the government, the State Bank of India (SBI) has taken the lead and become the first commercial bank in India to set up a mutual fund. The fund, called SBI Mutual Fund, intends to offer a diversified investment portfolio to subscribers with tax free incomes. The fund launched on September, 1st. 1987 with an amount of Rs. 100 crores, is both income and growth oriented. The fund shall be managed by the bank's wholly owned merchant banking subsidiary SBI Capital Market Ltd., and will invite subscription for seven years. It is a close ended fund for a fixed amount and for a specific period. Two way prices, namely bid and offer prices, are proposed to be quoted by the fund periodically to ensure liquidity to the subscribers with a wide choice of investment. Unlike units it would not listed on the stock market but traded over the counter. This is expected to save the investor heartburns following the eventuality of the units being quoted below par. These recent developments augur well for future financial development on capital market in India ....

RBI Guidelines

Reserve Bank of India has recently announced guidelines governing the functioning of Mutual Funds to ensure their orderly working and inspire investor confidence. Some of the important features of the guidelines are as follows :

1. All Mutual Funds shall be constituted under the Indian Trust Act.
2. An 'Arms Length' relationship shall be maintained between sponsor banks and those who manage the funds so that there is no clash of interests between the sponsor bank and beneficiaries.
3. Sponsor bank shall have stake equivalent to 1 per cent of the fund.
4. Investment objectives shall be made clear to the investing public.

5. Mutual Funds shall not undertake lending and money market operations. However, temporary investment in money market instruments is permitted.
6. Speculation through short sales/purchases is not permitted.
7. Investment in other Mutual funds is not permitted.
8. With a view to spread risk, any one single scheme shall not hold more than 5 per cent of the subscribed capital or debenture stock of any company. In case of more than one scheme of the Mutual fund, total shall not exceed 15 per cent.
9. Total investment in any one fund shall not exceed 15 per cent of the scheme fund.
10. Spread between purchase and sale shall not be more than 15 per cent.
11. Income distribution shall not be made on the basis of revaluation.

Conclusion

The above compelling arguments in favour of Mutual Funds clearly reveals that mutual funds can be ideally suited to Indian financial environment. It is a fund which can be tailored to suit every purpose to cove the entire spectrum of investment population requirements, in the country. The Government of India is encouraging such institutions through many amendments in : Banking regulation Act, Securities contract Act, Companies Act, Controller of Capital Issues Act and Securities Exchange board of India (SEBI) in April 1991, to help in increasing the investment by the general public on the one hand and the corporate sector in getting their capital requirements with little difficulty.

The recent Dave Committee report also emphasises on the participation of Mutual fund, investment clubs, venture capital banks and companies in Stock Exchange activities as a very important activity in providing stability to the market by reducing volatility of share prices. This is because these institutions are in a position to diversify and manage wider portfolios, take longer perspective as compared to individual investors. Thus, in India the USA model of financial institutions seems to have tremendous scope and positive role to play in raising the resources through capital market. But, if this US model is inefficiently managed by poor professional management, it will lead to misinvestment of funds and disastrous results and thus would not meet the developmental requirements of our country.

References

1. Ojha, P. D. "Capital Market-emerging Trends", *RBI Bulletin*, Bombay, January, 1988.
2. Hussain Abid, "Redesigning Industrial Investment Strategy", *Financial Express,* Bombay, August 28th, 1989.
3. Mayya, M. R. "Recent Developments in Stock Exchanges in investment"; A seminar organised on 'How to mange portfolio Investment, Canbank financial Service Ltd. Bombay, September, 19, 1987.
4. Dave, S. A; "Tex of Dave committee Report", *Economic Times,* (Bombay) 17t Oct., 1987, P. 4.
5. Ravi Shanker; "Capital Market", *Business World,* March 2-15, 1987, pp. 65-72.
6. Sambamurthy, B;"Mutual Funds", *The Charatered Accountant,* Vol XXXVIII No. 8, February 1990 PP. 688-670.
7. Avagol Malti; "Merchant Bankiing: "Emerging Areas in Indian Context" *Journal of Inter University Council for Business Education and Research,* Jan–June, 1990; Vol. 1, N. 1, pp. 30-36.

3

Mutual Fund in India A Financial Service in Capital Market

Nalini Prava Tripathy

The Indian capital market has been increasing tremendously during last few years. With the reforms of economy, reforms of industrial policy, reforms of public sector and reforms of financial sector, the economy has been opened up and many developments have been taking place in the Indian money market and capital market. In order to help the small investors, mutual fund industry has come to occupy an important place. The main objective of this paper is to examine the importance and growth of mutual funds and evaluate the operations of mutual funds and suggest some measures to make it a successful scheme in India.

Introduction

According to Shakespeare 'out of this nettle, danger, we pluck this flower, safety'. The economic development model adopted by India in the post-independence era has been characterised by mixed economy with the public sector playing a dominating role and the activities in private industrial sector regulated by various control measures enunciated from time to time. The industrial policy resolution was introduced by the government in the 1948, immediately after the independence. This outlined the approach to industrial growth and development. The Industrial policy statement of 1980 focussed attention on the need for promoting competition in the domestic market, technological upgradation and modernisation. A number of policy and procedural changes were introduced in 1985 and 1986, aimed at increasing productivity, reducing costs, improving quality, opening domestic market to increase competition and making free the public sector from constraints. Overall, in the seventh plan period (1985–86 to 1989–90), Indian industries grew by an impressive average annual rate of 8.5 percent. The last two decades have seen a phenomenal expansion in the geographical coverage and financial spread of our financial system. The spread of the banking system has been a major factor in promoting financial intermediation in the economy and in the growth of financial savings. With progressive liberalization of economic policies, there has been a rapid growth of capital market, money market and financial services industry including merchant banking, leasing and venture capital. Consistent with this evolution of the financial sector, the mutual fund industry has also come to occupy an important place.

Origin

Mutual funds go back to the time of the Egyptians and Phoenicians when they sold shares in caravans and vessels to spread the risk of these ventures. The foreign and colonial government Trust of London of 1868 is considered to be the forerunner of the modern concept of mutual funds. The USA is, however, considered to be the Mecca of modern mutual funds. By the early - 1930s quite a large number of close - ended mutual funds were in operation in the U.S.A. Much latter in 1954, the committee on finance for the private sector recommended mobilisation of savings of the middle class investors through unit trusts. Finally in July 1964, the concept took root in India when Unit Trust of India was set up with the twin objective of mobilising household savings and investing the funds in the capital market for industrial growth. Household sector accounted for about 80 percent of nation's savings and only about one third of such savings was available to the corporate sector. It was felt that UTI could be an effective vehicle for channelising progressively larger shares of household savings to productive investments in the corporate sector. The process of economic liberalization in the eighties not only brought in dramatic changes in the environment for Indian industries, Corporate sector and the capital market but also led to the emergence of demand for newer financial services such as issue management, corporate conselling, capital restructuring and loan syndication. After two decades of UTI monopoly, recently some other public sector organisation like LIC (1989), GIC (1991), SBI (1987), Can Bank (1987), Indian Bank (1990), Bank of India (1990), Punjab National Bank (1990) have been permitted to set up mutual funds. Mr. M. R. Maya the Executive Director of Bombay Stock Exchange opined recently that the decade of nineties will belong to mutual funds because the ordinary investor does not have the time, experience and patience to take independent investment decisions on his own.

Importance of Mutual Fund

Small investors face a lot of problems in the share market, limited resources, lack of professional advice, lack of information etc. Mutual funds have come as a much needed help to these investors. It is a special type of institutional device or an investment vehicle through which the investors pool their savings which are to be invested under the guidance of a team of experts in wide variety of portfolio's of Corporate securities in such a way, so as to minimise risk, while ensuring safety and stready return on investment. It forms an important part of the capital market, providing the benefits of a diversified portfolio and expert fund management to a large number, particularly small investors. Now a days, mutual fund are gaining its popularity due to the following reasons :

1. With the emphasis on increase in domestic savings and improvement in deployment of investment through markets, the need and scope for mutual fund operation has increased tremendously. The

basic purpose of reforms in the financial sector was to enhance the generation of domestic resources by reducing the dependence on outside funds. This calls for a market based institution which can tap the vast potential of domestic savings and channalise them for profitable investments. Mutual funds are not only best suited for the purpose but also capable of meeting this challenge.

2. An ordinary investor who applies for share in a public issue of any company is not assured of any firm allotment. But mutual funds who subscribe to the capital issue made by companies get firm allotment of shares. Mutual fund latter sell these shares in the same market and to the promoters of the company at a much higher price. Hence, mutual fund creates the investors confidence.

3. The psyche of the typical Indian investor has been summed up by Mr. S. A. Dave, Chairman of UTI, in three words; Yield, Liquidity and Security. The mutual funds, being set up in the public sector, have given the impression of being as safe a conduit for investment as bank deposits. Besides, the assured returns promised by them have had great appeal for the typical Indian investors.

4. As mutual funds are managed by professionals, they are considered to have a better knowledge of market behaviours. Besides, they bring a certain competence to their job. They also maximise gains by proper selection and timing of investment.

5. Another important thing is that the dividends and capital gains are reinvested automatically in mutual funds and hence are not fretted away. The automatic reinvestment feature of a mutual fund is a form of forced saving and can make a big difference in the long run.

6. The mutual fund operation provides a reasonable protection to investors. Besides, presently all schemes of mutual funds provide tax relief under section 80 L of the Income Tax Act and in addition, some schemes provide tax relief under section 88 of the Income Tax Act lead to the growth of importance of mutual fund in the minds of the investors.

7. As mutual funds creates awareness among urban and rural middle class people about the benefits of investment in capital market, through profitable and safe avenues, mutual fund could be able to make up a large amount of the surplus funds available with these people.

8. The mutual fund attracts foreign capital flow in the country and secure profitable investment avenues abroad for domestic savings through the opening of off-shore funds in various foreign investors. Lastly another notable thing is that mutual fund are controlled and regulated by SEBI and hence are considered safe. Due to all these benefits the importance of mutual fund has been increasing.

Schemes of Mutual Funds

Within a short span of four to five years mutual fund operation has become an integral part of the Indian financial scene and is poised for rapid growth in the near future. Today, there are eight mutual funds operating various schemes tailored to meet the diversified needs of savers. UTI has been able to register phenomenal growth in the mid eighties. Now there are 121 mutual fund schemes are launched in India including UTI"s scheme attracting over Rs. 45,000 Crores from more than 3 Crore investor's account. Out of this closed-end scheme are offered by mutual fund of India to issue shares for a limited period which are traded like any other security as the period and target amounts are definite under such schemes. Besides open-end scheme are lunched by mutual fund under which unlimited shares are issued by investors but these shares are not traded by any stock exchange. However, liquidity is provided by this scheme to the investors. In addition to this off-shore mutual funds have been launched by foreign banks, some Indian banks, like SBI, Canara Bank etc. and UTI to facilitate moment of capital from cash-rich countries to potentially high growth economics. Mutual funds established by leading public sector banks since 1987-SBIMF, Can Bank, Ind Bank, PNBMF and BOIMF, emerged as major players by offering bond like products with assurance of higher yields. The latest schemes of BOI mutual fund goes to the extent of allowing each individual investor to choose the date for receiving the income. Besides the bank mutual funds have also floated a few open-ended schemes, pure growth schemes and tax saving schemes. The LIC, GIC mutual funds offer insurance linked product providing various types of life and général insurance benefits to the investors. Also the income growth oriented schemes are operated by mutual fund to cater to an investor's needs for regular incomes and hence, it distributes dividend at intervals.

Growth Trends of Mutual Fund

Opening of the mutual fund industry to the public sector banks and insurance companies, led to the launching of more and more of new schemes. The mutual fund industry in India has grown fast in the recent period. The performance is encouraging especially because the emphasis in India has been on individual investors rather in contrast to advanced countries where mutual funds depend large on institutional investors. In general, it appears that the mutual fund in India have given a good account of themselves so far. UTI's annual sale of units crossed Rs. 1000 crores mark in 1986 to 1987, 2000 crores mark in 1987-88 and reached Rs. 5500 crores mark in 1989 to 1990. During 1990 to 91 on account of decline of corporate interest, sales declined to Rs. 4100 crores though individual sales increased over its preceding year. LICMF has concentrated on funds which includes life and accident cover. GICMF provide home insurance policy. The bank sponsored mutual fund floated regular income, growth and tax incentives schemes. Together the eight mutual fund service more than 15 million investors with UTI alone holds for 13 million unit holding accounts. Magnum Regular Income Scheme 1987 assured a return of 12 percent but gave 20 percent dividend in 1933. UTI record 26 percent dividend for 1992 to 93 under the unit 1964 scheme. Magnum Tax saving scheme 1988 to 89 did not promise any return but declared 14 percent dividend in 1993 and recorded a capital appreciation of 15 percent in the first year. Equity oriented scheme have earned attractive returns. Especially since early 1991 there has been a stready increase in the number of equity oriented growth funds. With the boom of June 1990 and then again 1991 due to the implementation of new economic policies towards structure of change the price of securities in stock market appreciated considerably. The high rate of growth in equity price led to a high rate of appreciation in the net asset value of the equity oriented funds for which investors started changing their preferences from fixed income funds to growth oriented or unfixed income funds. That is why more equity oriented mutual funds were launched in 1991. Master share provide a respective dividend of 20% per cent in 1993-94, Can share earned a dividend of 15 percent in 1993. In general the Unit Trust of India which manages over 28,000 crore under various schemes has an excellent reputation for its services.

Shortcomings in Operation of Mutual Fund

The mutual fund has been operating for the last five to six years. Thus, it is too early to evaluate its operations. However one should not lose sight to the fact that the formation years of any institution is very important to evaluate as they could be able to know the good or bad systems get evolved around this time. Following are some of the shortcomings in operation of mutual fund.

1. The funds are of externally managed. They do not have employees of their own. Also their is no specific law to supervise the mutual fund in India. There are multiple regulations. While UTI is governed by its own regulations, the banks are supervised by Reserve Bank of India, the Central Government and insurance company mutual funds are regulated by Central Government regulations.

2. At present, the investors in India prefer to invest in mutual fund as a substitute of fixed deposits in Banks. About 75 percent of the investors are not willing to invest in mutual funds unless there was a promise of a minimum return.

3. Sponsorship of mutual funds has a bearing on the integrity and efficiency of fund management which are key to establishing investor's confidence. So far, only public sector sponsorship or ownership of mutual fund organisations had taken care of this need.

4. Unrestrained fund rising by schemes without adequate supply of scrips can create severe imbalance in the market and exacerbate the distortions.

5. Many small companies did very well last year, but mutual funds can not reap their benefits because they are not allowed to invest in smaller companies. Not only this, a mutual fund is allowed to hold only a fixed maximum percentage of shares in a particular industry.

6. The mutual fund in India are formed as trusts. As there is no distinction made between sponsors, trustees and fund managers, the trustees play the roll of fund managers.

7. The increase in the number of mutual funds and various schemes have increased competition. Hence it has been remarked by Senior Broker "mutual funds are too busy trying to race against each other". As a result they lose their stabilising a factor in the market.

8. While UTI publishes details of accounts about their investments but mutual funds have not published any profit and loss account and balance sheet even after its operation.

9. The mutual fund have eroded the financial clout of institution in the stock market for which cross transaction between mutual funds and financial institutions are not only allowing speculators to manipulate price but also providing cash leading to the distortion of balanced growth of market.

10. As the mutual fund is very poor in standard of efficiency in investors service; such as despatch of certificates, repurchase and attending to inquiries lead to the detoriation of interest of the investors towards mutual fund.

11. Transparency is another area in mutual fund which was neglected till recently. Investors have right to know and asset management companies have an obligation to inform where and how his money has been deployed. But investors are deprived of getting the information.

Future Outlook and Suggestion

As mutual fund has entered into the Indian Capital market, growing profitable enough to attract competitors into this cherished territory encouraging competition among all the mutual fund operators, there is need to take some strategy to bring more confidence among investors for which mutual fund would be able to project the image successfully. The followings are some of the suggestion.

Firstly— As there is no comprehensive law to regulate the mutual fund in India, uniform co-ordinated regulations by a single agency would be formed which would provide the shelter to the investors.

Secondly— as the investors are not willing to invest in mutual fund unless a minimum return is assured, it is very essential to create in the mind of the investors that mutual funds are market instruments and associated with market risk hence mutual fund could not offer guaranteed income.

Thirdly— all the mutual funds are operated in the public sector. Hence private sector may be allowed to float mutual funds, intensifying competition in this industry.

Fourthly— due to operations of many mutual fund, there will be need for appropriate guidelines for self-regulation in respect of publicity/advertisement and inter-scheme transactions within each mutual fund.

Fifthly— the growth of mutual fund tends to increase the shareholdings in good companies, give rise the fear of destabilsing among industrial group, hence introduction of non-voting shares and lowering the debt-equity ratio help to remove these apprehension.

Sixthly— as there is no distinction between trustees, sponsors and fund managers, it is necessary to regulate frame work for a clear demarcation between the role of constituents, such as shelter, trustee and fund manager to protect the interest of the small investors.

Sevently— steps should be taken for funds to make fair and truthful disclosures of information to the investors. So that subscribes know what risk they are taking by investing in fund.

Eightly— infrastructure bottlenecks will have to be removed and banking and postal systems will have to be taken place for growth of mutual funds.

Ninethly— mutual funds need to take advantage of modern technology like computer and tele communications to render service to the investors.

Lastly— mutual funds are made by investors and investors interest ought to be paramount by setting standard of behaviours and efficiency through self-regularisations and professionalism.

Conclusion

With the structural liberalisation policies no doubt Indian economy is likely to return to a high grow path in few years. hence, mutual fund organisations are needed to upgrade their skills and technology. Success of mutual fund however would bright depending upon the implementation of suggestions.

References

1. Anagol, Malati & Katoli, Raghavendra, "Mutual Funds : just five year old and ready to run at a gallop" *Economic Times,* Febbruary 27, 1992.

2. Shukla, Sharad, "Mutual Funds : Past Performance is no Indicator of the Future" *Economic Times,* June 6, 1992.

3. De, Mainak, "Mutual Funds & Institutions - Paying to a different tune" *Economic Times,* June 15, 1991.

4. Dave, S. A., "Mutual Funds : Growth and Development" The *Journal of Indian Institute of Bankers,* Jan-march, 1992.

5. Bhatt, M. Narayana, "Setting standards for Investor Srvices" *Economic Times,* December 27, 1993.

6. *State Bank of India, Monthly Review,* Agust 1991, December 1991.

7. Marketman – Vol. 1, June 1992.

8. *Business India,* October 15-6, 1990.

9. Vyas, B. A., "Mutual Funds – Boon to the Common Investors" *Fortune India,* July 16, 1990.

10. Chandra, Prasanna, *The Investment Game* Tata Mc. Graw-Hill publishing, New Delhi.

11. Vyasaswy, N. J. *"Personal Investment and Tax planning Year Book"* Vision Books, New Delhi.

12. Ramola K.S., *"Mutual Fund and the Indian Capital Market" Yojana,* vol. 36, No. 11, June 30, 1992.

4

Mutual Funds in India - A Bird's Eye View

Bibhuti B. Pradhan

Indian economy and the Indian Capital market in particular, have recorded unprecedented growth and dynamism during the decade of eighties. Capital market chanelises the long term funds directly through securities market and indirectly through the mutual funds. In last five years the mutual funds activity has picked up significantly and gave a new dimension to the Indian capital market. The industrial liberalisation and financial liberalisation of this decade gave a new trend to the mutual funds, an excellent instrument for the mobilisation of savings of the middle class too. Table 1 shows a comprehensive analysis of different components of new issues market in India and observes that the role of mutual funds become an unique due to capital appreciation with the assistance of professional management and of diversified portfolio.

Table 1

Funds Raised form the New Issue Market (Rs. in crores)

	1985-86	*1986-87*	*1987-88*	*1988-89*	*1989-90*
(a) Shares	899.20 (30.09)	1009.00 (17.96)	1110.00 (16.56)	1020.00 (9.28)	1060.00 (6.85)
(b) Debentures	843.50 (28.22)	1556.00 (27.70)	664.00 (9.90)	2133.00 (19.40)	4656.00 (30.09)
(c) PSU Bonds	354.00 (11.85)	1791.00 (31.89)	2739.00 (40.85)	2498.00 (22.72)	4494.00 (29.04)
(d) Mutual Funds	891.75 (29.84)	1261.07 (22.45)	2191.42 (32.69)	5343.10 (48.60)	5263.73 (34.02)
Total	2988.45 (100.00)	5617.06 (100.00)	6704.42 (100.00)	10994.10 (100.00)	15473.73 (100.00)

What is a Mutual Funds

Mutual funds are specialised institutions that collectively manage the funds obtained from different investors through portfolio of securities and earn income through dividend, interest and capital gain. These specialised institutions are managed by professionals and have safety, liquidity and returns to the investors.

The concept of mutual funds, which prevail to day can be traced with the Foreign & Colonial Government Trust of London in 1868, and by 1930 it got momentum in the United States of America and later on spread to Italy, Japan, Germany, Canada, Austria, Mexico and Latin America. In India, the largest mutual fund was created with Unit Trust of India in 1964 to encourage savings and investment and participation in the income, profits and gains from the acquisition, holding, management and disposal of securities. At present there are mutual funds institutions in India to provide the benefit of diversified portfolios and expert investment advice and management to large number of investors. Table 2 shows the structure of mutual funds in India.

Funds	*Year of incorporation*	*Trustee*	*Investment manager*	*Custodian*	*Settler*
1. UTI	1964	UTI	UTI	UTI	UTI
2. SBI Mutual	1987	SBI Capital Market	SBI Capital Market	SBI	SBI
3. Canbank	1987	Canara Bank	Canbank Mutual	Canbank Mutual	Canara Bank
4. LIC Mutual	1989	Stock Holding Corp. of India	LIC Mutual	SHCI	LIC
5. Indbank Mutual	1989	Indian Bank	Indbank Mutual	Indian Bank	Indian Bank
6. P N B Mutual	1990	PNB Caps	PNB Caps	PNB	PNB
7. GIC Mutual	1990	SHCI	GIC Mutual	SHCI	GIC
8. BOI Mutual	1990	BOI FIN.	BOI FIN	BOI	BOI

Types of Mutual Funds

Mutual funds are comprises of different funds, whereas each funds are divided into equal units. The mutual funds mobilise savings of people from time to time for productive capital. The savers, which are called as fund holders or investors are better protected through mutual funds schemes through a group of professionals who manages the funds by way of diversified investment portfolios. Thus the investors are free from investing directly in large number of securities. there are different types of mutual funds scheme for diverse investors to fulfil their choices. Some of them are as follows ;

(i) Open-ended and Closed-ended Funds

Open ended and closed ended funds are identified on the basis of period/and or target amount of investment. If the period is fixed, it is called closed ended fund and if indefinite, called as open ended. Till March, 1990, UTI has offered 23, SBI Mutual 5, Canbank Mutual 6, LIC Mutual 3, Indian Bank Mutual 2 closed ended fund, whereas UTI offered 6, Canbank Mutual and LIC Mutual two each open ended scheme to the investing public. The closed ended funds are generally listed in the stock exchange, whereas opened ended funds are available to investors at any time from the mutual fund organisation on Net Asset Value (NAV) Master share of UTI, Canshare of Canbank Mutual are listed in the stock exchange and Unit scheme 1964 of UTI Cangilt and Cancigo of Canbank Mutual are of open ended funds.

(ii) Income and Growth Oriented Funds

These are specific investment objective funds on the basis of growth and balanced income within the open ended or closed ended funds. When investor invest in funds with a objective of yielding fixed return regularly it becomes income oriented funds. Monthly income unit scheme with Extra Bonus Plus growth (13), 1989 of UTI, Magnum monthly Income Scheme 1989 of SBI Mutual and Cancigo of Canbank Mutual are of income oriented funds. The institution generally take investment strategy by deployment of investors in fixed income yielding securities, when investors defer the liquidity of their investment with appreciation and risk with a hope of better return, it becomes a growth fund. Growing Income Unit Scheme, 1990, of UTI, Cangrowth and Candouble of Canbank Mutual, Ind Ratna of Indian Bank Mutual and Double [2] plus of Bank of India are of Growth oriented funds. In growth funds, the mutual fund institution generally diversify these investment in equity share with a hope of achieving large capital gain in future, If the funds need to meet both objective of growth and income simultaneously, it becomes a balanced or income-cum-growth funds -year monthly Income Unit Scheme with yearly Bonus and Growth 1990 of UTI, Can stock of Canbank Mutual, Swarna Puspa of Indian Bank Mutual, PNB Regular Income Plus, 1990 of PNB mutual, Dhanavarsha of LIC Mutual, Rising monthly Income Scheme of Bank of India are example of balanced or income-cum-growth funds. In these cases the funds are invested in diversified portfolio, i.e., equity share, debentures, PSU bonds, government securities and loans and advances.

(iii) Domestic and International Fund

One the basis of area of operation the funds can be domestic funds or international fund. domestic funds are available for the country investors, where as international funds are for international investor for off-shore countryman. All funds issued by mutual fund institutions are of domestic funds except India fund, 1986, India Growth Funds, 1987 of UTI, and India Magnum fund of SBI, which were floated in UK. and USA respectively, Besides, Citi Bank also launched an international fund for NRI investor in 1989-90.

(iv) Tax Saving and Non-tax Savings Funds

The funds floated by the mutual fund can be related to tax planning. The mutual funds schemes of various institution have attracted the investors to the great extent. Under 80 C of Income Tax Act, ULIP Scheme, under 80CC, Dhan 80CC of LIC Mutual, MTSS 1990 of SBI, Can 80CC, 1990 of Can bank Mutual and were become more popular among the tax-payers for their tax planning. The Equity linked Savings Scheme (ELSS) become more popular in 1990-91 and a number of closed-end funds fluctuated by UTI, SBI Mutual, Canbank Mutual, and PNB Mutual and by which the investor tax payers are eligible for deduction also 80C of Income Tax Act, with a condition of holding the fund for a minimum lock-in-period of three years. The other scheme of the mutual funds are of non-tax savings scheme.

(v) Specialised Funds

There are specialised funds available with the mutual fund organisation. They are with a specialised objective and for specialised interest. Venture Capital Unit Scheme (VECAUS) is of specialised open ended fund floated by UTI and ICICI and managed by the Technology Development and Information Company for financing small and medium size project of high-technology. Specific funds to developed by State Government, Central Government, Corporation and local authorities from time to time, which is not under this preview. From, April 12, 1991, RBI allow money market mutual funds (MMMFs) Scheme to be operated by the scheduled commercial bank and their subsidiaries to provide an additional short-term avenue to investors and thus bring money market instruments within the reach of individuals. This MMMFs will offer the investors dual benefit of high yields and safety on principal.

Regulatory Framework

The team of professionals always thinks for their credibility through greater responsibility towards their clients investors. The government and their representative bodies try to develop an uniform regulatory standard for better understanding among the investors and giving a healthy trend to the capital market. Thus the mutual funds of India too govern through Act, guidelines issued by the controlling bodies. The oldest and biggest mutual fund of India, UTI, govern by UTI act 1964 for their constitution and management pattern; investment policies and objectives; investment limits; pricing and income distribution pattern and above all for disclosure of accounting statements and policies. When the public sector banks started floating mutual funds schemes, the Reserve Bank of India issued guideline for the public sector bank mutual funds for their smooth functioning. At the later stage, the Government of India, Ministry of Finance had issued guidelines for mutual funds in June, 28, 1990 to set uniform rules for mutual fund organisation and to provide adequate safeguard to investors on establishment, management, investment objectives and policies; investment limitation; disclosures, pricing and valuation; distribution policy and statement of accounts. The Government of India authorised Securities and Exchange Board of India to accept registration of mutual funds and prescribe accounting and disclosure standards for the funds.

Investment Pattern

The funds collected by the mutual funds are invested in different portfolios, such as, equity shares, debentures, loans and advances, government securities, PSU bonds and others. The UTI guideline indicates that the funds can engage itself in holding or disposing of securities, collecting and discounting bills of exchange, purchase and sell of participation certificate in relation to any loan or advance granted by any public financial institutions or schedule bank, keeping of money and deposits with company, invest in securities floated by the Central Government, formulated scheme in association with LIC and or GIC, acquire immovable property, provide investment advisory and portfolio management service and any other kind of business authorised by the Ministry of Finance from time to time. UTI guideline restricts on not to invest more than 20% of the funds in any scheme and not to borrow more than 10% of the funds (NAV) for payment of dividend or meeting temporary situation if any.

On the other hand RBI restricts the public sector banking mutual funds not to engage in lending, underwriting, portfolio management and money market operations, but to enhance the activities of capital market by way of government or trustee securities, shares and debentures, of companies, and public sector bonds. RBI also restricts the mutual fund organisation not to invest more than 25% of total investible fund in money market instalments. The Government of India guideline on investment objectives and policies restrict not to invest more than 5% of its assets in share of any company under any scheme and in any other mutual fund organisations in exceptional cases for a temporary period within a ceiling of 5% of its assets. Government of India specified that any purchase of scrips must be on the name of fund and not to go for deposits with companies or other corporate bodies. In case of borrow of money or pledge of asset in emergency the mutual funds organisation should be reported to SEBI. Table 3, indicates the investible funds with the investment pattern of some leading mutual funds.

Table 3
Investment Pattern of Three Leading Mutual Funds of India

	UTI Mutual Fund	*SBI Mutual Fund*	*Canbank Mutual Fund*
Investible funds at 31st March, 1990 (Rs. in crores)	15892.49	540.00	522.95*
Investment Pattern (%)			
Equity	19.8	19.1	19.7
Debentures	21.3	43.1	28.6
Term loans and Deposits with companies	41.1	N. A.	8.8
Government Securities	18.8	3.3	16.9
PSU Bonds	N.A.	24.4	8.9
Others	26.0	10.1	7.1

* at December 1989

Conclusion

It gives a clear picture that mutual funds in India are safe, yielded better return and liquidatable for the investors point of view and on the other hard mobilises the savings of household sector for productive investment for other sector. SEBI is authorised to developed the accounting and disclosure standards for the mutual funds. The investor's are keen in observing the new instrument developed by the professional management team of different mutual funds. As another side of a coin the private sector and foreign ban are waiting for government approval to start with mutual funds scheme. By this way the Dr. F. A. Meheta, Chairman, the Investment Corporation of India said, "Mutual funds will be the wave of future ... it will represent an excellent instrument for the mobilisation of savings of the middle class", The mutual funds should enter into stock exchange and regulatory framework should be developed for listing criteria to render more confidence to the investors, because the investors are putting their eggs in one basket.

References

1. Annual Report 1988-89, Investment Corporation of India
2. Annual Report 1989-90, Unit Trust of India
3. Goyal, Madan, (1989), Mutual Funds in India, *State Bank of India Monthly Review,* June, Vol/XXVIII, No. 6.
4. Karap. N. P. (1990), Mutual Funds, *PNB Monthly Review,* June, Vol. 12, No. 6.
5. Mathew, T, (1991) Money Market Mutual Funds Rich Pickings, *Economic Times,* Calcutta.
6. Mutual Funds, (1990), *Capital Market,* 2–15, March, vol. IV, No. 25
7. Mutual Funds (1989), *Fortune India,* Aug. Vol. VII, No. 10
8. State of Capital Market 1989-90, Securities and Exchange Board of India, Bombay.

5

Capital Adequacy Norms in Banks Some Critical Issues

Dr. K. Satyanarayana

The subject of capital adequacy has been a major concern of regulatory/supervisory authorities of banks all over the world. Economic reforms in general and financial reforms in particular further propelled the need for Indian banks to fall in line with BIS standards which also stand endorsed by Narasimham Committee.

In an earlier article* I have dealt at length about the fundamental aspects of the concept, rationale and the norms of capital adequacy, etc. In this paper in the first part I intend to critically look at the RBI prescription and its time table of capital adequacy norms. In the second section the implications of its implementation for Indian banks are studied.

Part I RBI Prescription

BIS standards

In order to impart stability and soundness to the international banking system, the Cooke Committee, set up under the aegis of Basle-based Bank for International Settlements (BIS), had developed in 1988 a conceptual framework for measuring capital adequacy and capital

* Capital Adequacy Norms for "Sound Banking" PNB Monthly Review, March, 1991.

standards to be achieved particularly by internationally active banks. This struck the cord in regulatory/supervisory agencies of other countries. The norms, defined in terms of the risk weighted assets, were accepted not only by the banks in the G-10 countries but other countries also started accepting and adopting them.

RBI Time Table

In the light of the Basle-framework of capital standards and also as per the recommendations of Narasimham Committee, the Indian regulatory authority, i.e., the Reserve Bank has also started ringing the bell for adoption of capital standards and thus induced a process of strengthening the capital base of banks in India.

The RBI guidelines envisage a two-tier capital structure similar to BIS-framework, with a different timetable as indicated below according to the category of banks including the foreign banks operating in India. Ultimately, all banks would have to achieve a minimum of 8 per cent ratio as recommended by BIS though the banks who are confined to domestic operations have been given a four year gestation period upto March 1996 by RBI.

A) BIS time table

7.25 per cent by end 1990

8.0 per cent by Dec. 1992

B) RBI time table

Category of bank	*Target (%)*	*To be achieved by end March*
(i) Foreign banks operating in India	8	1993
(ii) Indian banks with branches abroad	9	1994
(iii) Other Indian banks (not having foreign branches)	4 (Tier 1 minimum 50%)	1993
	8	1996

Weightage Pattern of RBI

Tier I is the 'core' capital and tier II is 'supplementary' capital with the latter limited to a maximum of 100% of Tier I, as propounded by the Basle-framework. The risk weightage system as adopted by the RBI and given below briefly is more or less on the pattern of the BIS-framework.

Risk Weightage Pattern Suggested by RBI

Assets	*Risk weight (%)*
I. Fund based	
- CRR, SLR, govt. guaranteed assets, cash, claims on commercial banks, etc.	0
- Other fund based assets	100
II. Non fund based	
- Non fund assets counter guaranteed by govt. both Central and State	0
- Documentary LC (backed up by underlying shipments, etc.)	20
- Clean LC/LG & Other such commitments	50
- Financial guarantees/commitments	100

The detailed risk weightage pattern prescribed by RBI is given in Annexure B.

The RBI Framework

The framework as adopted by the RBI, after a brief consultative process with the bankers, is rather rigid and without much deviation from the BIS framework though the latter provided for some discretion to the respective national supervisory authority.

Equity Investment in Subsidiaries

As per the RBI guidelines, Tier I capital is to be taken net of all intangible assets, losses and equity investments in subsidiaries. Deduction from equity alongwith any cross holdings of capital of banks is advocated by the Basle-framework for such subsidiaries which are not consolidated for the purpose of capital adequacy. The objective was to avoid double gearing and thereby a sort of window dressing of capital. The normal practice is to consolidate subsidiaries for the purpose of assessing capital adequacy of banking groups while the RBI has not stipulated any such consolidation. This deduction stipulation will certainly affect the ratio of the parent bank as is illustrated below for one of the nationalised banks as on 31.3.1991.

	Parent Bank	*Subsidiary*	*Consolidated*
	(1)	*(2)*	*(1+2)*
A. Capital & Reserves	327	30	357
B. Risk Weighted Assets	9462	238	9700
C. Capital to Risk Weighted Assets Ratio (%)			
(i) Without deducting invt. in subsidiaries (A/B)	3.46	12.60	3.68
(ii) After deducting invt. in subsidiaries (as per RBI guideline)	3.14		

In the absence of any consolidation of accounts, does the RBI stipulation simply that the liabilities of the subsidiaries are to be met out of the capital and/or profits of the parent bank? In lieu of the above example it is better to consolidate balance sheets and work out the capital adequacy ratio. Alternatively, let there be separate capital adequacy norms for the subsidiaries and the equity investment be treated as 100 per cent risk asset for the parent bank.

Pattern of Weights

Claims on government backed loans

The RBI envisages 100 per cent risk for al loans except that guaranteed by Government of India/state governments. It means Central and state governments are treated on par with each other which may not be a true reflection of their financial strength, liquidity and fiscal prudence. Some differential weightage in favour of Central Government backed loans is weightage in favour of Central Government backed loans is warranted. Similarly, there are many private sector companies which carry better liquidity and profitability levels than the government backed public sector undertakings. Is it not ironical to find that an advance to a sick public sector unit backed by state government guarantee and not yielding any income to the bank is treated as a zero risk asset while advance to a cash rich private sector company (or a public sector one not guaranteed by the government) is treated at 100% risk?

Rating of the company (whether public or private) by institutions like CRISIL, ICRA, etc., should be the basis for differential risk weightage pattern rather than whether it is backed up by a government guarantee or not. This is more so in case of state governments which are reputed for not honouring their guarantee commitments when called for.

Loans against government securities

Similarly loans against government securities such as NSCs, Indira Vikas Patras and other gilt-edged securities can be treated at par with loans backed by government guarantees (with low risk) and hence can be given a lower risk weightage than 100% weightage envisaged by RBI.

Pension payment

Pension disbursed to the debit of suspense account are basically claims on the central government or state government as the case may be and as such should be treated as zero or low risk assets whereas RBI circular treats them as 100 per cent risk assets under "other assets".

Staff loans

Staff loans do not carry any risk as they are adjusted either in the normal course or through terminal benefits. Certainly they can't be treated at 100 per cent risk as envisaged by RBI.

Income Recognition and Asset Classification Vs. Capital Adequacy

The approach of RBI for income recognition and asset classification introduced recently is a welcome though a long overdue measure from the point of view of international standards especially in the context of opening up of our economy. However, it brings certain contradictions when we interpolate it with the risk pattern suggested by RBI. For example, a loan guaranteed by state government is treated as zero risk asset for capital adequacy purpose. But from the operational point of view it may be under health code 4 or 5 where it is treated as non performing asset. Thus, a non-performing asset can be a zero risk asset and performing one can be 100 per cent risk asset. Such a situation arises due to the difference in the approaches. For capital adequacy the approach is *Counter Party Failure* and for income recognition and asset classification it is *Conduct/Operation* of the account.

Uniform Time-Table

Though the approach of RBI is equitable in prescribing higher capital for banks with high risk-assets profile, the uniform time-table may not be practicable since the size and financial strengths of banks differ widely. The time table for all domestic banks (without international presence)is uniform, i.e., 1993-96. Probably it is too far fetched to ignore the size and financial strength of each bank while fixing the time targets. Similarly, for banks with even one or two branches abroad the time target of 1994 is also too short unless fresh capital is invested either by the government or through market intervention. Differential approach based on realistic assessment of each bank's financial strength may be a feasible proposition in this regard after spelling out the strategies including the augmentation policy if any by the government.

Discipline of Capital Adequacy

What will happen if a bank is not able to adhere to the capital adequacy norms prescribe by RBI within the stipulated time frame? RBI's circular dated 22-4-92 is silent about any punitive measures for erring banks who will not be able to augment the capital and reserves base to the required levels. However, positive incentives are suggested in the recent policy guidelines of branch licensing wherein those banks who fulfill the capital adequacy norms will have some liberty to open specialised branches without prior permission of RBI, etc. Regulatory authorities in the global context are pursuing a more rigid and rigorous approach in this regard. Reports appearing in the international press indicate that banks face thereat of closure in case they fail to comply with capital adequacy norms within the target date. Apart from the pressure from regulatory and supervisory authorities for adherence of capital adequacy norms, banks who intend to operate in international market have to achieve these minimum standards or else they will not be able to have entry or survive in the competitive market.

Part II Implications of Implementation of Capital Adequacy Norms for Bank

Additional Capital Requirement

Laudable as the objective is, what with the low capital base, most of the Indian banks would fall short of the norms with glaring gaps. Rough estimates for public sector banks indicate a gap of Rs. 870 crores @ 4% norm) as on March 1991 and assuming an annual average growth rate of 14% in risk weighted assets, these banks may require to mobilize additional Rs. 20,000 crores within the five year period ending 1996 as shown in the table at Annexure A. Generating the additional capital of this dimension throws into sharp focus the issue of asset-liability management.

Augmenting Capital Base

There is no ready-made recipe. The dimension of the gap is such that major policy changes are required to achieve the proposed standards. The options could be :

Govt. contribution

Since 1985, Govt. has contributed about Rs. 2, 600 crores to equity capital of nationalised banks. However, the gap remains large. Given the resource crunch of the government and its policy to restrict both fiscal and budget deficit in the face of low dividend pay-out by the banks to the govt. it may not be able to fill the gap.

Increase in profits

A greater part of the profits may be used to pattern the capital base. Though this cannot be underscored, the present levels do not warrant for such optimism. The gross profit ratio of public sector banks is around 1.4% of working funds. Assuming, an annual increase of 15% in deposits and other liabilities and 50% of the increased asset portfolio to be in the 100% risk category, profits would be required to increase 0.4 to 4.5% of working funds for filling up the envisaged gap. Given the existing profit curve this would imply a steep upward kink which may not be feasible. In the face of new guidelines on income recognition and provisioning, further strain on profits is inevitable.

Raising Funds Through Market

With the liability of government to inject fresh capital sooner or later it will have to open the doors to public participation. The process for other public sector undertakings has already started, then why not for banks? The extent of privatisation will depend on pace of economic restructuring, ability to overcome trade union resistance and degree of public confidence in the professional approach and financial strength of the banks.

Securitisation

This would imply selling of the loan assets and in effect it would amount to shedding off the high-risk advances. Thus, the bank is relieved of all the risks attached to the securitised asset and also the need to hold capital in support of its assets to the extent it sells or securities its asses. In India the securitisation process is in its infancy and is yet to become popular in the banking system. Introduction of ARF as recommended by Narasimham Committee is also a step in this direction.

Secret Reserves and Revaluation Reserves

Some of the banks may be carrying latent and/or other general reserves which may qualify for Tier II for the purpose of capital adequacy. Probably with the introduction of new format of balance sheet from March 1992 such secret/latent reserves must have been brought to the surface and incorporated in the balance sheet. However, certain banks still have some cushion in the form of provision not required but made as an abundant precaution such as depreciation provision on core investments, etc. Further, it is widely accepted that some of the assets on banks' balance sheet which are still at historical costs, need to be revalued, especially 'premises'. A rough estimate of such reserves potential can be obtained by taking the book value of premises and multiplied 4-5 time. For public sector banks as on 31st March 1991 roughly it works out to a revaluation reserve of Rs. 1,500 crores after taking a discount factor or 0.5% for any plausible forced sale of such premises as envisaged in the BIS-framework.

Restructuring Through Capital Adequacy

Many suggestions have been made on restructuring of Indian commercial banks. Practically every exercise on a relook at the banking system ended up with some recommendation or other on restructuring. Unfortunately, very little of it could find a practical shape. Some of the reasons for such an impasse may be trade union resistance and lack of political will. It is also possible that the rationale suggested for restructuring must not have been very convincing and adequate enough for the policy makers to accept and implement.

In case the Indian commercial banks are not able to individually achieve the said standards of capital adequacy, it may be worthwhile to examine whether collectively a few of them can achieve them. In such an eventuality it may pave the way for the overdue implementation of restructuring of the banks on the lines suggested by various expert groups including the latest by Narasimham Committee.

Exposure Limits and Capital Adequacy

Media is agog with scam news. Not a day passes without some news or other about scam in the Indian securities market. Can we say that if capital adequacy norms are implemented in India we could have averted the scam ? Perhaps not! But certainly it could have prevented players like Bank of Karad and Metropolitan Co-operative Bank to play beyond their capacity in the market. It is because of their dismally low capital adequacy ratio that they are not able to recoup/repay the losses inflicted on other innocent players in the market while NHB, SBI and foreign banks were able to recoup/provide instantaneously notwithstanding the claims and counter claims between them. Prescription of exposure limits and suitable mechanism to monitor would have certainly prevented the embarrassment the regulatory/supervisory authorities are facing in the scam scenario. *Capital adequacy level should be certainly one of the criteria to fix the exposure limits* for players in the money and capital markets in due course.

Applicability to Finance Institutions

This brings into focus as to why capital adequacy norms are talked about only for banks in India and not for financial institutions. It may be due to the fact that financial institutions do not come under the regulatory purview of RBI. Hence, RBI has restricted its implementation of capital adequacy norms to banks only.

In fact the European Economic Community in BRUSSELS is pursuing an initiative (parallel to what Bank for International Settlement was doing with regard to capital adequacy norms) to develop a common solvency ratio to be applied to all credit institutions in the community. Probably it is time for us in India to extend capital adequacy norms on international pattern to all financial/credit institutions both at Central and State level.

Capital Adequacy – not a Ratio but a Philosophy

Traditionally, banks have an insatiable thirst for deposits. Can you think of a situation where a banker can say, "I can't absorb any more deposits". What will happen to a banker with low capital adequacy ratio? Can he afford to take more deposits especially in a liberalised situation unless he is sure of its deployment :

(i) in a profitable manner, and

(ii) without disturbing the capital adequacy ratio adversely.

In other words productivity and profitability are crucial to bank for maintaining the requisite capital adequacy ratio prescribed by RBI.

Thus, capital adequacy is not simply a ratio but a philosophy. Every time you are trying to increase the deposit-resource base on the liability side of the balance sheet conscious attempt has to be made to invest it either in (i) low yielding and low risk liquid asset like CRR and SLR items or (ii) in high yielding and high risk loan assets.

The vicious ad tricky situation develops when a banker tries to go in for more of low risk category assets for meeting the capital adequacy. In doing so he will end up with low profits which again pulls down the numerator (networth of the bank) of the ratio. On the other hand if he tries to till his balance in favour of the high risk assets he may end up with high proportion of not only high risk assets (inflating the denominator) but also face inherent increase in non-performing assets which ultimately may reduce his profit margin and thereby the net worth. Thus, implementation of capital adequacy norms is going to radically change the outlook of bankers and will force them to weigh each of their transaction in a commercial and professional manner rather than leaving them to be accidental or mechanistic.

Need for Trimming the Balance Sheet

The balance sheet format for banks has been changed from March 1992, and they are coming out with their statement of affairs in the new transparent format. Banks should not treat the balance sheet as a year end exercise of an accountant. The philosophy and approach of bankers to the business should be reflected in it. What should be the right proportion of assets from both the risk point of view and yield point of view is no doubt going to be their major concern in the days to come. What is equally important is the plan to reduce the high risk and non-performing miscellaneous assets incorporated in balance sheet under different nomenclature in banks. Due to lack of awareness or due to outmoded accounting practices banks are carrying many asset items in the balance sheet which could have been otherwise accounted in profit and loss account.

Uniform Accounting System

It is reported that certain Indian banks who applied for a licence to open a subsidiary in UK were asked by the Bank of England to mobilize a start up capital of 16% as against a minimum 8% of BIS standard. What can be the reason for such a situation ? It is that our accounting systems and asset classifications are not at par with international standards ? Thanks to the recent measure taken by RBI on asset classification and income recognition on the pattern recommended by Narasimham Committee, doubts are raised by bankers whether it will be feasible to introduce at this stage such accounting system even in a phased manner spread over 3 years. Nevertheless, banks cannot postpone any more its implementation if they want to remain competitive both domestically and internationally.

Management Information System

There may be instances in banks where due to lack of availability of proper data the assessment of risk weighted assets may be on the high side. For example, advances against deposits are to be netted from the risk weighted assets for assessing the capital adequacy ratio. Banks undertake to pay at par refund orders, dividend warrants, etc., after accepting deposits from corporate clients. But such payments at various branches may be made to the debit of either suspense or general advances head wherein one may not be able to decipher from the balance sheet what is the actual amount of such payment/advances backed by deposits from the corporate client thereby resulting in estimation of inflated level of risk weighted assets.

Thus, availability of requisite MIS data to arrive at the accurate capital adequacy ratio is also essential. There is lot of information which may not be available in the balance sheet which goes into the estimation of capital adequacy ratio. The exact amount of cash margins against which non-fund based exposures are committed, non-fund based commitment counter guaranteed by Govt., amount of advances against bank's own deposits, etc., are a few of the examples which are not revealed in the balance sheet nor information is available at corporate level. MIS of the bank has to be re-oriented to incorporate such details.

Monitoring by RBI

Annual reports of the banks should incorporate information about the capital adequacy levels vis-a-vis the norms. Both RBI and Govt. of India have already started calling for information on the requisite formats from banks but it is better if such monitoring is under RBI only.

Awareness of the Concept at Grass Root Level

The concept of capital adequacy is new and awareness level among banks is very low at present. Except for peripheral level of awareness, the concept, the content and its implications have not yet reached even the senior executives in the banking industry. It is high time that apex level institutes like NIBM, Central Staff Colleges and training centres of banks conduct short duration programmes or seminars on this subject so that the message spreads to the zonal/regional and even branch level. It is ultimately realization at these levels which can lead to higher profitability necessary to improve the capital and reserve base. The concept of asset classification and income recognition can also be combined with capital adequacy issues while conducting such seminars and programmes. The business meetings, conferences, etc., at Head Office, Zonal and Regional level should also include in their agenda strategic discussion on the implementation ad achievement of the same.

Summary and Conclusions

The subject of capital adequacy for commercial banks has assumed greater significance due to rapid metamorphosis of financial markets and the consequent competitive environment in which they are placed both internally and in the international market. In the first part of this article an attempt is made to have a critical look at the Reserve Bank of India guidelines on capital adequacy norms and in the second part some policy implications to the bankers are raised.

The Reserve Bank of India issued detailed guidelines to all the commercial banks recently vide their D.B.O.D. circular dated 22nd April 1992 regarding computation of capital adequacy ratio and the differential time table for achieving the targeted ratio of 8% by 1996. The Reserve Bank of India has neither spelt out any rationale behind the time table nor any strategy for achieving the requisite ratio by the targeted dates. Uniform time table for all the domestic banks seems to be unrealistic especially when there is a vast heterogeneity of financial strength among them. The Reserve Bank of India has also not spelt out what punitive action will it contemplate if a bank does not achieve the requisite ratio by the targeted time frame.

Deduction of equity investment in the subsidiaries of the banks from the capital base of the parent bank pulls down drastically the capital adequacy ratio of the parent bank. Either consolidation of the balance sheets of the subsidiaries with parent bank or alternatively prescribing capital adequacy norms separately for subsidiaries may be a more rational approach.

The weightage pattern suggested by Reserve Bank of India has several inconsistencies in applying the risk principle of "counter party failure" as suggested by Basle-framework. Notable among them are zero risk weightage for even state government guaranteed loans and 100% risk on assets which are essentially claims on the government either directly or indirectly in the form of pensions reimbursable, loans granted against government securities, etc. In the long run it is better to move towards risk weightage pattern based on the credit rating of the borrowal account.

Public sector banks as a group have to increase their capital base from Rs. 5840 crores as on March 1991 to around Rs. 20,000 crores by 1996. This is a stupendous task and appears to be beyond their reach as per the existing trends of growth in business and profits unless specific strategies like market intervention, securitiesation, re-valuation of assets, etc., are resorted to besides any contribution from the government which is most unlikely in the present context of their attempts to reduce the fiscal deficit.

Implementation of capital adequacy norms raise certain issues for bankers, regulators and policy makers. Continued impasse on restructuring the banks can be resolved by making capital adequacy norms as one of the main criteria to do the restructuring of the banks. Regulators can make use of the ratio as the basis for fixing exposure limits to banks so that there is little possibility for banks to play beyond their capacity as happened in the recent 'scam'. It is high time that the capital adequacy norms are also made applicable and enforced on financial institutions both at all India and state level.

Once the capital adequacy norms are implemented the bankers will be forced to give up directed and regimented system and follow a professional approach by adopting cost benefit analysis for most of their transactions/operations. Even they have to think of trimming their transparent balance sheets in such a way that they depict the true picture of their revenue and thereby the profits and reserves positions. It is also interesting to see how banks will cope up with the new accounting norms introduced by RBI for income recognition and asset classification, on one hand, and capital adequacy, on the other, where the inherent approaches and assumption are such that attempts to implement the former may result in pulling down the latter.

Both the Reserve Bank of India and the Banking division of Govt. of India have started monitoring separately the implementation of the norms. It is in the interest of the system to have such monitoring role restricted to RBI alone in which case the banks will be in a better position to respond by developing proper MIS and thereby avoiding duplicacy and redundancy.

The concept of capital adequacy being new, the awareness levels among banks is low. it is high time the efforts are made by training agencies like MIBM, training network of banks and other financial institutions t take up the role of spreading the philosophy, explain the system of computation and help in evolving strategies to achieve the set task of capital adequacy. It is also essential to bring in such awareness even at the grass root level along with the new concepts of income recognition and asset classification through the regular business meetings, conferences and training programmes. It is ultimately realisation at these levels which can lead to higher profitability which is a vital prerequisite in the long run to achieve a healthy ad competitive capital adequacy ratio.

Annexure A

Projection for Capital Adequacy for Public Sector Banks

Year	*Capital reserves*	*Estimated risk weighted assets*	*Required capital & reserves*		*Gap w.r.t. 1991 levels of capital & reserves*	
			For 4%	*For 8%*	*4%*	*8%*
	(i)	*(ii)*	*(iii)*	*(iv)*	*(v)*	*Vi)*
			(ii x 4%)	(ii x 8%)	(iii–i)	(iv–i)
1991	5840	167733*	6709	13419	869	2579
1992	–	191216	7649	15297	1809	9457
1993	–	217986	8719	17439	2379	11599
1994	–	248504	9940	19880	4100	14040
1995	–	283295	11332	22663	5492	16823
1996	–	322956	12918	25836	7078	19996

* Based on estimated ratio of 3.48% (source : NIBM Seminar on the Report of the Committee on the Financial System, February 1992)

Notes (i) Risk weighted assets are projected to increase at an annual average rate of 14%

(ii) Only tier I capital is taken into account

Annexure B

Risk Weightage Pattern Prescribed by RBI (Vide DBOD Circular dated 22/4/1992)

I. Domestic Operations

A) Funded risk assets	Percentage weight
(i) Cash, balances with Reserve Bank of India, balances with other banks, money at call and short notice and investments in Government and other trustee securities	0
(ii) Claims on commercial banks such as certificates of deposits, etc.	0
(iii) Other investments	100
(iv) Loans and advances including bills purchased and discounted and other credit facilities	
(a) Loans guaranteed by Govt. of India	0
(b) Loans guaranteed by state Govts.	0
(c) Loans granted to public sector undertakings of Government of India	100
(d) Loans granted to public sector undertakings of state Govts.	100
(e) Others	100
(v) Premises, furniture and fixture	100
(vi) Other assets	100

Notes :

1. Netting may be done only for advances collateralised by cash margins or deposits and in respect of assets where provisions for depreciation of for bad and doubtful debts have been made.
2. Equity investments n subsidiaries, intangible assets and losses deducted form Tier I capital should be assigned zero weight.

(B) Off-Balance sheet items

The credit risk exposure attached to off-Balance sheet items has to be first calculated by multiplying the face amount of each of the off-Balance sheet items by the "credit conversion factor" as indicated in the table below. This will then have to be again multiplied by the weights attributable to the relevant counter party as specified above.

	Instruments	Credit conversion factor (per cent)
(i)	Direct credit substitutes, e.g., general guarantees of indebtedness (including standby letters of credit serving as financial guarantees for loans and securities and acceptances (including endorsements with the character of acceptances)	100
(ii)	Certain transaction-related contingent items (e.g. performance bonds, bid bonds, warranties and standby letters of credit related to particular transactions)	50
(iii)	Short-term self-liquidating trade-related contingencies (such as documentary credits collateralised by the underlying shipments)	20
(iv)	Sale and repurchase agreement and asset sales with recourse, where the credit risk remains with the bank	100
(v)	Forward asset purchases, forward deposits and partly paid shares and securities, which represent commitments with certain drawdon	100
(vi)	Note issuance facilities and revolving underwriting facilities	50

(vii)	Other commitments (e.g., formal standby facilities and credit lines) with an original maturity of over one year	50
(viii)	Similar commitments with an original maturity up to one year, or which can be unconditionally cancelled at any time	0
(ix)	Aggregate outstanding foreign exchange contracts of original maturity—	
	– less than one year	2
	– for each additional year or part thereof	3

Notes :

1. Cash margins/deposits shall be deducted before applying the conversion factor.
2. After applying the conversion factor as indicated above, the adjusted off-Balance sheet value shall again be multiplied by the weight attributable to the relevant counterparty as specified in I–A above.

6

Factoring Service in Indian Financial System

Nalini Prava Tripathy

The last two decade has witnessed considerable diversification of the money and capital market. New financial services and instruments have appeared on the scene. And for the growth of industrial output and management of sales, timely collection of debt and receivable has become more significant. Thus the factoring service have been introduced to eliminate the unduly delay and provide immediate cash payment to the suppliers. In this paper an attempt has been made to highlight the conceptual framework of factoring, progress of factoring in India and suggest some approach for which the factoring service would be able to penetrate and expand their market.

Introduction

The growth and evolution of financial markets in India since the 1950s can be viewed in three broad phases. The first two decades of the 1950s and 1960s constituted a phase of transition. The period from 1969 to 1985, spanning a decade and a half, can be called the period of expansion and diversification. The period since 1985 has been marked by consolidation, innovation and liberalisation. The last two decades have seen a phenomenal expansion in the geographical coverage and financial spread of our financial system. The development of the financial sector is a major achievement and it has contributed significantly to the increase in our savings rate, especially of the household sector. A financial system essentially comprises financial institutions, instruments and markets which together provide the necessary frame work for mobilisation and allocation of savings. A vibrant, efficient and innovative financial system is the key to the rapid and sustained growth of the economy.

The capital market and money market are considered to be the most important segment of the financial system. The capital market has undergone significant transformation and has witnessed an explosive growth in terms of its size, number and variety of scrips issued and listed on the stock exchange. Similarly the money market have also opened up and witnessed the arrival of new money market instruments like 182 days treasury Bills, certificates of Deposits, commercial paper and participation certificates. To encourage bill financing and develop bill culture, the bill discounting rate have been reduced. The bill rediscounting market has been widened by allowing more participants to re-discount bill. As the debts are not collected in time and are handicapped by lack of sufficient working capital, the production and expansion of business is affected. Hence the working group on money market, that is, Vaghul Committee, recommended introduction of factoring services in India to solve the financial problems of the small scale supplies. Reserve Bank of India then appointed a committee under the chairmanship of C. S. Kalyanasundram, former Managing Director of the State Bank of India to examine the feasibility of factoring service in India and suggest operational modalities of launching such a service. The factoring services have been introduced to ease the problems of collection of debts and delayed payments from the debtors.

Origin

The origin of factoring can be traced during the 15th and 16th centuries in England and France which were exporting goods to their colonies and required an agency to distribute the goods, provide funds and collect the proceeds. In 19th and 20th centuries, such agents only provide funds and collection of sale proceeds. Thus the factoring was introduced in the developed countries in U. K. and USA and at present the USA and European countries account for nearly 90 percent of global factoring turnover. Factoring is of a recent origin in the Indian context. In 1988, the Reserve Bank of India constituted a High powered Committee to examine the scope for offering factoring service in the country. In 1989, the committee directed that factoring activities could be undertaken by banks through the medium of separate subsidiaries.

Concept of Factoring

The word 'factor' has been derived from the Latin word "Facere" which means 'to make or do' i.e. to get things done. The Webster Dictionary states that 'Factor' is an agent as a banking or finance company, engaged in financing the operations of certain companies. The Oxford Dictionary defines the term 'factor' as a person or an organisation acting as a business agent. According to C. S. Kalyana Sundaram "Factoring is the outright purchase of credit approved account receivables with the factor assuming bad debt losses" According to Alan Gilpin "Factoring is a system designated to eliminate payment risk in overseas sales and ensure that the seller receives prompt settlements'. According to Biscoe "Factoring may be defined as a continuing legal relationship between a financial institution (the factor) and a business concern (the client) selling goods or providing services to trade customers (the customer) an open account basis. Whereby the factor purchases the clients book debts (account receivable) either without or with recourse to the client and in relation there to controls the credit extended to customers and administers the sales ledger". According to Financial Executives Hand book" The term describes another specialised and important form of credit and collection service. It is essentially the extra service of credit protection that differentiates factoring from accounts receivable financing". In simple words factoring can be defined as an arrangement under which the factor purchase the account receivables and makes immediate cash payment to the suppliers. The factor undertakes the responsibility of collecting the dues from the buyer hence assumes risk. For this type of services as well as for the interest, he charges a fee for intervening period technically known as factorage. Table 1 depicts the process of factoring.

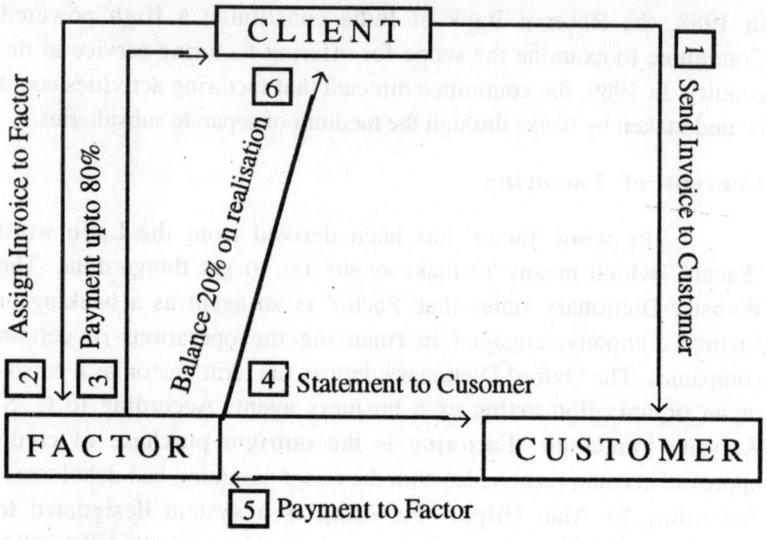

Description

Transaction No.

1. The client sell the good on credit basis to customer.
2. The client offers the assigned invoice to the factor.
3. The factor makes a pre-payment upto 80% of the value of the assigned invoices.

4. The factor notifies the customer sending a statement of account.
5. Customer remits the amount due to the factor.
6. Factor makes balance 20% of the invoice value to the client when the account is collected or on a guaranteed payment date.

Types of Factoring

The Factoring can be categorised in the following types :

1. Notified and undisclosed Factoring

In case of notified factoring the customer is informed about the assignment of the debt to the factoring agent and also asked to pay the dues to the factor instead of to the firm. But in undisclosed factoring the factoring arrangement is not disclosed to the customer but the customer is required to make the payment to the changed address. This is also known as non-notified factoring or confidential factoring.

2. Resources and Non-resources Factoring

In resource factoring the factor purchases the receivables on the condition that the loss arising on account of irrecoverable, receivables will be borne by the client. While in non-resource factoring the bad debts are borne by the factoring agent. Since the factor bears the loss arising on account of irrecoverable debts, the factor charges a higher commission.

3. Advance and Maturity Factoring

In case of advance factoring, the factor provides an advance varying between 75-85 percent of the value of receivables factored and the balance is paid upon collection or on the guaranteed payment date. Whereas in maturity factoring, the factor makes the payment on a guaranteed payment date or on the date of collection.

4. Bank participation Factoring

Under this arrangement the bank finances against the reserves which is maintain by the factor on which the firm creates a floating charge on the factoring reserves in favour of bank and borrow against these reserves.

5. Invoice Factoring

Strictly speaking, this form of factoring is not considered as an integral part of the present day factoring system because it does not carry the service element of factoring. Under this type of factoring the debts due to the client are purchased by the factor who thus provides improved liquidity under which the supplier's position becomes very comfortable.

6. Buyer Based, Seller Based and Selective Factoring

Buyer based discounting would mean the factor would maintain a list of buyers and any would be factored without recourse to the seller. Whereas in seller based discounting the factor would prefer seller based discounting with resource and without recourse; seller based discounting is known as selective where the seller is restricted to sells to the approved buyer.

7. With Credit and Without Credit Factoring

The buyer can make a contract in favour of seller that the seller will not assign the credit to any third party. Under such circumstances, the factor will be unable to register his power of attorney and will have to trust the seller to remitt the money to him after realisation.

8. Export Factoring

This is also known as international factoring or cross-border Factoring. Export factoring house deal with export sales and provide financial service, collection service, advisory service and also provide service for completing legal formalities pertaining to export. Generally export factoring is quite helpful to small exporter and new entrants to export business in India.

Functions of the Factor

Finance

The factor provides advance money to the client against outstanding debt about 80 percent and the balance minus commission on maturity. Hence the factor acts as source of short term funds.

Debt Administration

Under this, the responsibility of the factor is to take care of all the function relating to the maintenance of the sales leader on open item basis which should clearly show all the outstanding invoices and the unallocated cash. The factor will send monthly statements of accounts and inform the client about the progress of collection of debts from time to time and also informs him about the debts collected and overdue accounts. This helps the client to increase his sales with availability of finance.

Credit Risk

One of the important function of the factoring is credit protection. The factoring organisation is required to ascertain the credit worthiness and feasibility position of several buyers and accordingly advice the client. Hence the client will be guided by the factor's advice in this regard, under which the factor reduce the risk of loss through bad debts.

Advisory Services

By virtue of their experience the factor also able to provide advisory service on credit and financial dealings and excess to extensive credit information. The factor can also advise customer on work load analysis, replacement programme on machinery and other technical problems.

Advantages

Factoring offers the following advantages from the clients point of views :

1. Through factoring the client gets immediate cash which reduces the operating cycle and increase the turnover.

2. As the factor takes all the responsibility of maintaining sales ledger administration, credit control and debt collection, the client is relieved from the administrative burden.

3. As the factor provides instant cash to the client against credit sales, the client can derive benefit from the cash discounts by making prompt payment for his purchases. This will substantially reduce purchase costs and improve profitability.

4. By off loading the Administration, the client has more time for planning, running and improving the business and exploiting opportunities.

5. Factoring ensures a perfect debtor turnover and improves the profitability of the client by avoiding the risk of bad debts.

6. The factor provides the information like credit-standing position of the customer under which the client can avoid easy poor quality and risky customer.

7. As the factor collects the accounts in time, there is no need for the client to spend its valuable time for slow paying customer under which there will be saving in interest payment contribute towards cost savings.

International Scene

Factoring has assumed greater importance in European countries even if it is quite popular in North America and Asia because factoring as an option to finance both similarly domestic and export business in Europe. Similarly Factoring has suffered in the business profile due to depressed economic situation in Europe. Also there has been merger of the factoring companies in US. However, despite all the factors in Europe, factors are not unduly worried about the long run prospects.

Factoring Turnover : 1991 : Selected Countries

	No. of Companies	Factoring Turnover ($ Billion)	%age Shame in World Factoring
Italy	80	75.0	28.9
U. S.	20	51.5	19.8
U. K	30	28.5	11.0
Mexico	70	18.5	7.1
Japan	43	16.5	6.4
France	17	15.0	5.8
Netherlands	5	11.0	4.2
Germany	14	10.1	3.9
South Korea	15	6.0	2.3
Sweden	20	5.0	1.9
Others.	–	22.9	8.8
Total	507*	260.0	100.0

* Relates to 1990

Source : Indian Institute of Banker's Journal July – Sept. 1993.

Year-Wise Factoring Turnover
($ Billion)

	1986	1987	1988	1989	1990	1991*
World domestic factoring	97.8	131.1	151.5	179.2	203.6	244.4
World International factoring	6.0	8.7	8.9	10.8	13.8	15.6
World Total	103.8	139.8	160.4	190.0	244.4	260.0

* Estimated

Source : Indian Institute of Bankers Journal, July –Sept. 1993

Among all the countries, italy ranked first in factoring turnover constitutated 28.9 percent share in world factoring turn over. As per the data on the above table, the total turnover in factoring business worldwide during 1991 aggregated and 260 billion which was higher 6 percent over the 1990 figure. In 1990, the world's factoring turnover is $ 44.4 which is more than 29 percent in the earlier years. Of the total $ 260 billion factoring turnover, export factoring turnover was only 6 percent and domestic factoring is 94 percent. Even if the factoring is recent phenomenon in Japan but it ranks fifth in terms of turnover consistuted nearly 6.4 prcent share in world factoring turnover. One of the important facture of the japaneese factoring market is that it focus on discounting of promissory notes. Now factoring is an business activity in Singapore, Malaysia and south Korea.

Two major global associations were formed in the sixties to promote international factoring. The international Factors Group which was formed in sixties is represented in more than 25 trading countries through out the world. The factor chains international is the other association was formed in 1968 consists of more than 90 independent companes operating in about 30 countries.

Indian Prespectives

In Indian context, factoring is being viewed as a source of short-term finance can offer useful services specially to the supplier. The introduction of factoring services in our country arises not only due to the limitation of the banking industry but on account of managing the receivable of the manufactures efficiently. Further the professional approach of factors in assessment of credit, debt collection, management of sales ledger may develop a healthy payment culture. So the factoring organisation should be set-up as a one monolithic institution to handle the entire business in the century. Factoring business has just started in India. The State Bank of India has started its subsidiary known as SBI factors and commercial services private limited with effect from 31st August 1991. It is operating in the western region. As per SBI factors first annual report (1991-92) it has on its books 25 units who are manufacturers and sellers of goods and 164 customers, 60 percent of the units are small scale units. They deal in chemicals, packaging plastics and allied products, consumer durables, castings pharmaceuticals and light engineering. At present, the Can Bank factors limited are operating in four Southern States and the union territories of Pondicherry and Lakshadweep. Similarly Uco bank, United bank of India and Allahabad Bank are to jointly set a factoring subsidiary in the Eastern part of India. The Punjab National bank is operating in Northern part of India. thus the introduction of factoring services in India is expected to give a boost to the Industrial production, employment and economic growth.

Suggestions

No doubt, factoring service is a new dimension in Indian Industries for the first time in an organised manner. There are many benefits of factoring which a firm can avail out of it. As India is in the process of opening up and liberalising its economy, where the financial service industry including factor has been growing tremendously, it is necessary to implement some of the suggestion for which the factoring service would able to penetrate and expand their own market. The following are some of the suggestions :

1. To make factoring economically viable, the Government should pass appropriate laws exempting factored debts from payment of stamp duty on assignment.

2. It is required to regulate prescribed norms for new entrants to factoring business.

3. Indian legislation does not deal with various aspects involved in factoring business. So it would be necessary to promote special legislation to establish efficient and viable factoring organisation.

4. For communication, computer support is essentially for factors for extending their services efficiently and economically.

5. The civil procedure code should be suitably amended facilitating recovery of factored debts through summary proceedings under order 37 of the code.

6. There are delinquent debts on account of insufficient budgetary provisions among government departments and large business undertakings of the public and private sectors. In such circumstances an environment factoring will be more effective.

7. The saving of financial loss is to be borne by industrial and business concerns on account of employing excess manpower hence credit discipline is needed for the success of factoring system in India.

8. There are no reliable credit agency in India to provide information like reputation, financial standing and business prospects of the customer which is considered to be one of the most obstacle for the success of factoring business in India. So even if the CRISIL is introduced, the RBI should take immediate measures to setup more agency in the economy.

Conclusion

The factoring companies must be allowed to have a debt capacity on par with the other intermediaries like leasing and hire-purchase companies, so that the companies can design co-efficient capital structure. No doubt factoring service will provide new dimension to achieve the goal of modernise India and also achieve the economic prosperity.

References

1. Factoring Service – A Boon to Small Scale Units, *The Economic Times, March,* 1990.

2. *The Economic Times,* February 26, 1990.

3. Bajaj K. K., "Factoring Service Make a doubt in India" *Financial Express,* August 20, 1991.

4. Bansal, L. K. : Factoring – Another Financing Source, *Chartered Secretary,* January, 1990.

5. Srikirshna, P., Factoring, *SBI Monthly Review,* August, 1988.

6. Brandemberg, M. : Why don't they use Factoring ? *Accountancy,* January, 1984.

7. Dandekar, M. N., The Financial System of Factoring – An Approach for Introduction in India, *SBI Monthly Review* March, 1991.

8. Subramanyam, M. J. Factoring Services – The Long – Awaited Financial Service, *Indian Banking Today and Tomorrow,* November 1991.

9. Pappu, Narasimham, "Factoring in India – A Note", *ASCI Journal of Management,* Vol. 20, No. 2–3 (Sept. – Dec., 1990).

10. Koppar, V. H., "Prospects of Factoring Services, *Yojana*, July 15, 1993.

11. Biscoe, P. M., "Law and Practice of Credit Factoring" 1975.

12. Kalyan Sundaram, C. S. "Factoring Services" *CBI Economic Bulletin* Vol. 11. March 1991.

13. *The Utkal Business Review*, vol. XI 1992–93.

14. Kaiswal, Dr. G.C.R., "Factoring Services in India". *The Banker 41* June 1993.

15. Sing, Balwinder, "Factoring Service in India : Progress and Prospects". *The Indian Journal of Commerce,* Vol. No. XLV, Part–II June 1992.

16. Dangwal, R. C. Nagi, K. S., Pandey, H. P., "Energence of Factoring Service in India : A Case *Study of Indian Commercial Banks" The Indian Journal of Commerce,* vol. No. XLV Part–II, June 1992.

17. Kochar, N. G., "International Factoring and Forfaiting" The *Journal of the Indian Institute of Bankers,* July – Septermber 1993.

18. *State Bank of India Monthly Review,* April, 1992.

7

Forfaiting – An Instrument of Export Finance

Nalini Prava Tripathy

India cannot improve its export finance if it is confined only to the domestic market. Therefore to remove this anomaly the RBI brings in abroad the forfaiting and discounting of export bills. Forfaiting is a technique mostly employed for financing goods on medium term deferred basis. It enables the exporter to convert a credit sale into a cash sale through process of discounting of export receivables. In this article an attempt has been made to highlight conceptual framework, operations, prospects and some suggestions to create more environment for the growth of forfaiting transactions to tap potentialities of India.

Introduction

"The craft of the merchant is to bring a thing from where it abounds to where it is costly" Emerson.

In most of the developing Countries various agencies like Commercial Banks, Export–Import Bank and the Export Insurance Bodies specialise in financing exports to importers situated in other Countries. But due to various reasons, the financial Institutions and other agencies are becoming inadequate terms for providing financial assistance. Further international banks are compelling to adhere strictly to the capital adequacy norms for which banks are finding difficulties to put extra funds in the risky line of business. At the same time, Letter of Credit which was considered at one time the best way of financing exports have the demerit of being transaction-oriented and not ideal in case of repetive transaction where fast delivery is required. So exporters receive delayed payment from importers which put them in difficulties to expand their export business. In consideration of having received the immediate payment, forfaiting concept would come as a boon for the Indian exporters as an alternative source of finance to ensure to keep international business expanding. Even if this method of finance is prevailing for more than 20 years in the international market, it is a recent development in India.

Conceptual Framework

The concept "Forfaiting" was originally developed in Switzerland in mid 60s and became important after the end of second world war with the objective of helping finance to the West German exports to Eastern block Countries. It is a technique to help the exporter to sell his goods on credit and yet receive the case well before the due date. Subsequently with the increased volume of trade between the developed and developing countries, forfaiting provides a suitable channel for grant of more flexible credit to the exporters under situation.

"Forfait" a french word means "to surrender something" or "give up one's right". Accordingly the exporters surrender his right to the forfaiter to receive future payment from the buyer to whom goods have been supplied. The exporters offer credit terms to the importer and then sale the debt to the forfaiter. Hence the forfaiter waives recourse to the exporter, if the importer defaults in payments. Forfaiting has emerged an extremely important tool for offering fixed rate term financing to an importer while retaining the benefits of a cash sale.

Sequence of Operations

Forfaiting is done without recourse means the forfaitor can not go back to the exporter for the recovery of the money which the importer may not pay him, when a forfaiting transaction is to be taken place between the exporter and forfaiter, it is an essential pre-requisite to explain detail informations like the nature of goods, prices, the currency and the name of the importer, guarantees etc. to the forfaiter. Then a contract is made between the exporter and importer specifying the payment would be made by the importer to the forfaiter. As a result, notes are signed by the importer and informed to his local bank. Then the importer's bank guarantees the notes and forward them to the exporter's bank with instruction to release them to the exporter's bank against shipping documents. The exporter ships the goods and gives the shipping documents to his bank under which the bank release the notes to the exporter and forward them to the importer through importeı's bank. The exporter presents the notes to the forfaiter and receive the cash.

Costs of Forfaiting

The cost involved in forfaiting can be classified as:

(i) discount fees towards providing the finance depend upon the risk content of the transactions. However, exporters are willing to pay extra 15 percent more for forfaiting due to additional services provided by the forfaiter. The forfaiter ordinarily charges a commission of about 1 percent of the face value of the receivable and if the exporter wants an advance against the receivables sold before then he is required to pay interest to the forfaiter on the amount of advance.

(ii) The cost is also involved in terms of front-end management fee to EXIM bank for handling the transaction.

(iii) A commitment fee is also charged by the bank normally upto one year for undertaking.

Benefits of Forfaiting

* The forfaiting provides service in such a manner to meet the needs of the exporters and importers. One of the greatest advantages of forfaiting is its simplicity and flexibility. forfaiting can be used to finance any export transaction. This technique is highly useful to medium term fixed rate financing.

* Since the transaction is without recourse basis, it helps the exporters convert their credit sale into a cash sale.

* Where the exporter's banker were not quick enough to provide additional credit limit for extending period, the forfaiting route with the advantage of a "fixed interest rate and no currency risk" could be an export facilitator.

* The biggest advantage with forfaiting is that exporters do not have to carry the receivables in their balance sheet.

* The exporters do not deal with the forfaiter. The EXIM bank is doing averring for him.

* Exporter is saved of all the hassles in collecting dues as it is once sold to the forfaiter, he is out of the transaction.

* Documentation procedure is simple, so it provides an opportunity to structure the deal.

* Forfaiting is a very good barometer of international risk profile. Therefore, now the Indian banks are allowed to discount their overseas customers bills without adding their name.

* Initially, forfaiting was used mainly for capital goods but now the situation has changed and the forfaiting company is now willing to look at smaller export orders too.

* Forfaiting provides a host of services such as checking the credit worthiness of the foreign buyer, extension of credit lines, advancing money against submission of invoices, sales ledger, administration etc.

Indian Perspectives

In India Commercial banks provide concessional finance for export transaction at both the pre and post shipment stages. Refinance is provided by the Reserve Bank of India and the Export–Import Bank of India against credit guaranteed by Commercial Banks. However, inspite of the schemes floated by commercial banks, only the large and well-established exporters are being benefited by this scheme and small exporters are facing difficulties in making arrangement for necessary funds. So forfaiting as an alternative instrument for export finance, introduced in March 1993 for the first time with the Export–Import Bank of India as the sole authorised intermediary which could help the Indian exporter. A specialist forfaiting company providing exporters and banks with the product of "discount of receivables or a without recourse basis". This instrument is very helpful to the exporters in Indian market and convert their medium to long term credit for the overseas buyers developing on the extent of risk attached to their individual countries by the forfaiting agency. Previously London-based Banquet Indosuez Aval looks for a minimum size for each transaction but now the forfaiting company willing to look at smaller export orders from India. Now about 15 to 20 percent of the forfaiting market today is represented by transaction involving commodity exports upto 180 to 360 days. Recently in November 1993 as per the guidelines of RBI, exporters are also eligible to avail of pre-shipment credit in foreign currency from commercial banks and which both the domestic and imported inputs of the goods exported form India. Therefore the exporter is able to avail of credit in foreign currency at both pre and post-shipment levels at internationally competitive rates. This would enable the exporters to quote competitive price for the exported goods which should help them to show better results in the exports in the years ahead.

International Players

Over a period of time forfaiting has become quite popular and it has cover all sorts of trade and countries. The important forfaiting centres are London, Zurich, Hong Kong, Singapore and Frank-Fort. Among the Europeans, it is an extremely acceptable form of transaction. Because it could offer both facilities like unlimited financial and total credit to the exporter and became a popular instrument in the world's financial service market. London is said to be the biggest market involved in forfaiting operations in the whole world. Also forfaiters are quite active in Paris, Geneva, Brussels, Vienna etc. Hence this illustrative list goes to show the importance that forfaiting has assumed in recent years.

Suggestions

Forfaiting is an instrument which facilitates a large number of technological opportunities for the creation and commercialisation of new goods and services. Thus efforts are required to create more environment for the growth of forfaiting transaction to tap potentialities of India. To ensure an effective forfaiting transactions the following measures may be taken.

* There should be a legal frame work for the forfaiting transaction.
* High risk like political, sovereign and commercial is involved in such transaction. This should be corrected.
* There is a lack of data base regarding importers as well as importing countries. So necessary action should be taken for encouraging forfaiting transaction.
* There is absence of secondary market. If this is accepted as reality there will be better market.
* When the exporter deals with a buyer from an overseas high country, the cost of service involved becomes high. So, there is a need for a change in out look.

* Exim bank would act as an intermediary between Indian exporter and a forfaiting agency abroad. So this instrument would normally be used for difficulties countries. Therefore specific modification is required in respect of Exim bank to involve in direct finance in such cases.

Conclusion

The exact structure of the financing is determined only by the needs and inventiveness of the exporter importer and forfaiter. As our country is more oriented towards an era of export promotion under liberalised economy system of which forfaiting has a very important role to play, undoubtedly forfaiting would be more brightened in India if these challenges are to be met more effectively.

References

1. Kocher, M. G., "International Factoring and Forfaiting" *The Journal of the Indian Institute of Bankers,* July-Septermber, 1993.
2. Balchandran, Dr. P., "PCFC Scheme" *The Journal of the Indian Institute of Bankers,* October-December, 1993.
3. Mohanty, Dr. A., "Forfaiting Position and Prospects", *State Bank of India a Monthly Review,* March, 1993.
4. *Sankalpa,* January–June, 1993.
5. Batra, Dr. G. S., Kaur, Narinder., "An alternative Source of Trade Financing". *Chartered Secretary,* July, 1993.
6. *Economic Times,* Jan. 21, 1994.
7. Nair, Kishore., "Financing of Long Term Export Receivables – Forfaiting"., *The Banker,* April, 1994.
8. Aruna, M., "Advantage Forfaiting" *Chartered Financial Analyst,* November, 1994.

8

Development Banks

Dr. Rita Mathur

The process of Industrial Policy reforms initiated with the announcement of New Industrial Policy in July 1991 was carried forward during the subsequent years. Deregulation ad simplification of procedures were extended to several industrial sectors. The other notable changes were opening up of oil exploration and power sectors to both domestic and foreign private investment; dual marketing system for liquefied petroleum gas and kerosene and decanalisation of their imports; and a five-year tax holiday for new projects for generation and distribution of power starting from the year of generation of power. The Government announced decontrol of phosphiatic fertilisers and molasses as also incentives for sugar and phosphatic fertiliser industries. The Government also announced five-year tax holiday (starting from the year of production) for new industrial undertakings set up in notified backward states.

Several additional measures were initiated during 1992-96 to encourage flow of foreign investment. India signed the Multilateral Investment Guarantee Agency (MIGA) protocol to provide protection to foreign investment. The Foreign Exchange Regulations Act (FERA) 1973 was substantially liberalised giving companies with majority foreign equity holding more freedom in their operations. All restriction on FERA companies for borrowing funds or raising deposits in India, taking over or creating any interest in business in Indian companies, establishing branches/liaison offices and acquisition of any undertaking or company in India (expect those engaged in agriculture and plantation) were removed. The Government allowed use of foreign trade marks for sales in the domestic market. The non-resident Indians (NRIs) and Overseas Corporate Bodies (OCBs) predominantly owned by them were allowed to invest up to 100% foreign equity in high-priority areas with full repatriation benefits. These and the earlier reform measures had an impact on the flow of Foreign Direct Investment (FDI) into the country. Approvals of FDI increased from Rs. 1328 crore in 1991-92 to Rs. 5611.2 crore in 1992-93.

The Government announced operational guidelines for setting up National Renewal Fund (NRF) with two components viz. National Renewal Grant Fund and Employment Generation Fund.

Financial Sector

Capital Market

The major developments in the capital market were the repeal of Capital Issues (control) Act, abolition of the Office of the Controller of Capital Issues and consequent introduction of free pricing of public issues. During the year 1991-96, there was a support in the number of capital issues entering the market as also the amount proposed to be raised. There were 1037 issues (prospectus and rights) for an amount of Rs. 19,825.6 crore. An important development was the introduction of innovative/hybrid instruments with special features to attract investors. IDBI entered the market to raise up to Rs. 400 crore through three debt instruments. ICICI too raised funds through issue of a debt instrument. The secondary market reached its peak at the beginning of the year; however, after the detection of the irregularities in the securities transactions and also due to the poor industrial corporate performance in the first half of 1992-93, the market had a subdued trend. With the inflow of funds from FIIs, and better corporate performance the secondary market is showing a significant up-trend.

The Government permitted foreign institutional investors (FIIs) to make direct portfolio investment in the Indian capital market. Up to November 1993, 118 FIIs have been registered with SEBI and US $ 650 ml have been invested by FIIs in the Indian companies stock. For the orderly functioning of the capital markets, the National Stock Exchange of India Ltd. (NSEIL) was incorporated by financial institutions and banks with IDBI as the nodal agency. The RBI has proposed the establishment of Securities Trading Corporation of India to provide a base for active secondary market in Government dated securities and PSU bonds. Measures were also introduced to promote the market makers who would specialise in buying and selling of securities by offering two-way quotations; RBI issued guidelines regarding bank financing of their operations. The overall climate for industrial investment remained buoyant and demand for funds continued to remain high till March 31, 1996 on the supply side, there was a perceptible decline in mobilisation of resources by the corporate sector from the capital market, both domestic and international, due to depressed market conditions. With RBI also reining in growth of broad money to moderate inflationary pressures liquidity conditions hardened and there was a corresponding sustained rise in the market clearing interest rates.

Development Finance

The financial sector is in the process of rapid change consequent upon structural adjustments initiated by the Government in various sectors of the economy. Steps were taken to implement financial sector reforms in a phased manner. In order to meet the challenges of the emerging competitive environment, financial institutions commenced new services/products and set up new organisations.

As part of the reform process, IFCI was reconstituted as a company under the Companies Act to impart higher degree of operational flexibility. IDBI introduced several new products and promoted new organisations to improve the functioning of the capital market. It set up a credit rating agency named Credit Analysis and Research Ltd. (CARE) and a company for registrar, transfer and custodial services called Investor Services of India Ltd. (ISIL). The Government also appointed IDBI as the nodal agency for establishing the National Stock Exchange of India. IDBI is also in the process of setting up a joint venture company with Asian Capital Partners, Hong Kong for investment banking services and is also setting up a commercial bank. ICICI set up ICICI Securities and Finance Company Ltd. (I-SEC) for investment banking operations and an Asset Management Company for its Mutual Funds. It is also in the process of setting up a company to offer registrar and transfer services, entering the business of stock broking and custodial services and setting up a commercial bank. IFCI also has plans to set up an asset management company for a mutual fund, a venture capital funds specifically for the auto components industry and a debenture trusteeship company. The investment institutions, especially UTI, are also planning to promote new ventures to diversify their activities. Several financial institutions are proposing to start commercial banks under the new dispensation announced by RBI for setting up banks in the private sector.

Guidelines were issued by RBI to commercial banks with regard to asset classification, income recognition and provisioning. The Government decided to contribute Rs. 5700 crore as additional capital to the nationalised banks. The RBI formulated guidelines to govern entry and operations of new private sector banks. The setting up of a Board for Financial Supervision in RBI was announced. The working group set up b RBI to make a in-depth study of the role of non-banking financial companies (NBFCs) suggested regulatory measures for ensuring their healthy growth, based on which guidelines were announced by RBI. The Government appointed a high-powered Committee (Chairman: Shri R.N. Malhotra) to make recommendations for reforms in the insurance sector.

Industrial Development Bank of India

The Industrial Development Bank of India (IDBI) was established on July 1, 1964 under an Act of Parliament as the principal financial institution for industrial finance in the country. IDBI provides assistance to the medium and large scale industries by way of a variety of products under direct finance, refinance of industrial loans and bills finance. IDBI also extends resource support to all-India and state-level financial institutions ad other financial intermediaries. Its wholly owned subsidiary, the Small Industries Development Bank of India (SIDBI) provides assistance to the small scale sector. In response to the growing needs of various segments of industry, IDBI, over the years, has diversified its range of products and services. Besides introducing new products such as asset credit, equipment finance, equipment leasing and bridge loans, IDBI also provides merchant banking and debenture trusteeship services to the corporate sector.

During the year, IDBI diversified its range of foreign exchange related products by offering forward cover to borrowers in respect of their debt service obligation to IDBI or payment against letters of credit which are backed by rupee loans from IDBI. It is now in a position to offer other liability management products such as interest and currency swaps, forward rate agreements, etc. to its borrowers.

IDBI re-oriented its institution-building activities and promoted several organisations to provide services for more efficient functioning of the capital market. it promoted the Credit Analysis and Research Ltd. (CARE), a credit rating organisation, in collaboration with financial institutions, commercial banks and finance companies. CARE has initially taken up credit rating of debt instruments and has plans to diversify into other areas such as information services and equity research in the near future. IDBI also set up Investor Services of India Ltd. (ISIL) in association with financial institutions and private sector consultants. ISIL will provide registrar and transfer services on par with international standards and would undertake custodial services.

IDBI is also in the process of participating in a joint venture company with Asian Capital Partners Ltd., Hong Kong, to undertake a full range of investment banking activities including corporate broking, financial advisory services and merchant banking activities. IDBI has been appointed the nodal agency for setting up of National Stock Exchange of India Ltd. (NSEIL). The NSEIL, being set up by the financial institutions and banks, is moving rapidly towards establishing the National Stock Exchange to provide comprehensive nation-wide, screen-based electronic trading facilities.

With a view to strengthening the State Financial Corporations (SFCs) to enable them to meet the challenges of the competitive financial system, IDBI, issued guidelines to SFCs to adopt the prudential norms in regard to income recognition, provisioning, etc. in a phased manner. It has also submitted a detailed action plan to the Government which covers management and organisation, operations, accounting policies and prudential norms, resource mix, re-capitalisation and training needs of SFCs.

Resource-raising Efforts— In a year characterised by tight liquidity conditions, a robust demand for industrial credit and consequently high and raising marketing clearing interest rates, mobilisation of adequate resources at cost effective rates took primacy of place in the Banks strategic plans. IDBI's efforts in this direction met with considerable success as it managed to mobilise nearly Rs. 10,500 crore from both equity and debt segments of domestic and international financial markets. The flexi-bonds issues, which closed on March 13, 1996 is a good barometer of the over-whelming investor responses to IDBI floated paper. This has amply demonstrated the appeal of innovatively structured investor-friendly instruments, efficient networking and at a more fundamental level, reflected the overwhelming and reassuring investor faith in IDBI's brand equity. The year 1995, also witnessed the largest public issue of equity by IDBI in India's capital market history. The over-whelming response to the issue in July 1995 which generated Rs. 1,942 crore, with the net public offer being oversubscribed 1.4 times.

The resources garnered from the domestic market were matched by sizeable funds raised from outside the country. During the year 1995, the Bank raised $ 50 million from international markets through a combination of syndicated loans, floating rate notes and a foreign line of infrastructure credit for £300 million from EXIM J, all contracted at competitive rates.

Strategic Focus— The Bank maintained its strategic focus on anticipating the challenges of this new liberalised era in finance and continued to provide increasingly diverse and sophisticated financial services of the highest quality to help its clients attain their business objectives. At the same time, the Bank also took steps to consolidate and build upon the early gains from its responses to the new deregulated environment.

IDBI's technology-driven commercial bank adjunct- the IDBI Bank Ltd.– became functional during the year and has so far opened four branches at Indore, Hyderabad, Chandigarh and Madras, while its plans for opening a further four branches are at an advanced stage of implementation. The Bank's stock broking subsidiary–IDBI Capital Market Services Ltd. (ICMS) - which commenced operations in March 1995, has emerged as a profit-earning entity from primary market operations in its maiden year and is planning to diversify into areas of equity research and wholesale debt. IDBI had set up a domestic Mutual Fund and an Asset Management Company in 1994-95 and the two schemes launched by them during the year, incorporating innovative features generated an encouraging response. The bank has initiated steps for setting up the country's first National Depository, in association with the Unit Trust of India and the National Stock Exchange. When in place, it is expected to impart the necessary depth to the capital market.

Organisational Improvement— IDBI recognizes that, in the emerging competitive environment, a constant review of strategic business plan, including organisational improvement and human resource development, will be key to its long term growth, keeping these objectives in mind, the Bank had appointed *Booz-Allen & Hamilton,* an international management consultancy firm, to take a look at its business strategy and organisation and indicate the required changes. The consultants have recently completed a diagnostic study. Further action on their recommendations for restructuring and organisational changes are under consideration.

Prospects— Demand for investment is expected to remain buoyant during years to come based on cumulative undisbursed loan sanctions and the stock of current and pending applications with the FIs. On the resources side, a series of steps taken by the monetary authorities – particularly, the serial reduction in CRR and SLR and recent relaxation in GDR and FCB guidelines - are expected to enhance liquidity, deposit growth and lendable capacity of financial intermediaries. FDI flows show clear signs of gathering momentum and appear likely to show a significant rise in the coming fiscal. Thus investment climate in the coming fiscal year looks promising on current reckoning.

The liquidity tightness that continued during current few years displaying some signs of easing, and short term money market rates are already evidencing signs of decline largely as a result of significant monetary policy changes effected by the RBI in April and July 1996. The long term rates, however, continue to rule firm and the trends in this regard need to be watched in the context of anticipated growth of industrial investment in general and infrastructural demand for credit in particular, complemented by the market borrowing programme of the government.

Infrastructure development is a key commitment on the country's macro agenda and, reflecting national priorities, IDBI too has adopted infrastructure financing as a key focus area. The fund requirements for financing projects in this sector are, however, of gigantic proportions. With the opening up of the sector to foreign investment, the focus seems to have shifted to attracting sizeable external funds for financing such projects. While it is no doubt important to attract as much foreign investment as possible, for which there is a good scope, there is a need to pay attention to resources required to be raised domestically, as bulk of the required fund flow into infrastructure has to be sources domestically.

In this context, there exists considerable urgency to put in place a meaningful long term debt market in the country to enable the corporate sector as well as FIs to raise long term funds. Recent debt issues by IDBI and a few other entities have shown strong investor preferences for debt instruments. In all mature markets bulk of long term funds is provided by Insurance Funds, Provident Funds, Superannuating Funds, and Gratuity Funds. In India, because of statutory restrictions, participation of these funds in the long term bond markets is not very significant. There is need to relax these restrictions which could given the bond market the necessary fillip.

It is heartening to note that the infrastructure sector has received due attention in the Budget proposals of 1996-97 and a series of measures have been announced by the Honorable Finance Minister for its development. The definitional ambit of infrastructure for the purpose of five-year tax holiday under Sec 80IA has been widened to include irrigation, water supply, sanitation and sewerage systems. With a view to improving the retail-level attractiveness of investing in infrastructure projects, all income from such investments has been exempted from tax. Infrastructure projects have themselves benefited by way of exclusion from payment of Minimum Alternative Tax. An adequately capitalised specialised financial institution for providing financial and other assistance to long-gestative projects in select infrastructure section constituents is proposed to be set up. It is hoped that the new organisation will bring additionality of resources to the sector and will not duplicate the efforts of existing DFIs in this regard.

Table 1

Assistance Sanctioned and Disbursed

(Rs. crore)

Year	Sanctions	Growth rate %	Disburse-ments	Growth rate %
1964-70	304.8	–	278.8	–
1970-75	738.6	–	559.5	–
1975-80	3364.3	–	2346.2	–
1980-81	1276.6	–	1014.1	–
1981-82	1525.7	19.5	1217.9	20.1
1982-83	1786.2	17.1	1498.5	23.0
1983-84	2312.0	29.4	1774.3	18.4
1984-85	3350.0	44.9	2073.7	16.9
1985-86	3491.8	4.2	2783.9	34.2
1986-87	4327.3	23.9	3205.9	15.2
1987-88	4580.6	5.9	3613.6	12.7
1988-89	6659.9	45.4	4745.8	31.3
1989-90	7495.8	12.6	5084.8	7.1
1990-91	6431.2	(-)19.9	4459.4	(-) 12.3 (26.9)
1991-92	7590.0	18.0	5762.8	29.2
1992-93	9459.4	24.6	6668.5	15.7
Cummulative up to end-March 1993	64,695.5		47087.7	

Notes: 1. Figures up to 1989-90 and cumulative up to end-March 1993 are inclusive of assistance to small sector.

2. Figures in brackets against the year 1990-91 indicate percentage change over assistance of 1989-90 excluding small sector.

Industrial Finance Corporation of India Ltd.

The Industrial Finance Corporation of India (IFCI) was established in 1948 under the Industrial Finance Corporation Act, 1948. It has now been converted into a limited company under the Companies Act, 1956 and has been notified as a company with effect from July 1, 193. Now it is known as The Industrial Finance Corporation of India Ltd. IFCI provides medium and long term finance to industry through a variety of products under project finance and financial services such as equipment leasing, equipment procurement, buyers' and suppliers' credit, finance to leasing and hire-purchase concerns, etc. IFCI also provides merchant banking services. Additionally, it helps industrialisation through wide ranging promotional activities.

During 1992-93, IFCI participated with other all-India financial institutions in promoting the National Stock Exchange of India Ltd. it has planned to set up an asset management company for a mutual fund, a venture capital fund specifically for the auto components industry and a debenture trusteeship company.

Industrial Credit and Investment Corporation of India Ltd.

The Industrial Credit and Investment Corporation of India Ltd. (ICICI) was set up as a public limited company in 1955 with Government support and active participation of the World Bank. The primary objective of establishing ICICI was to meet the foreign exchange requirements of industrial concerns and for promoting industries in the private sector. ICICI assists industries through a range of products under project finance by way of rupee and foreign currency loans, underwriting/direct subscription to equity/debentures, guarantees and under financial services such as asset credit, deferred credit, equipment leasing, instalment sale, etc.

During 1992-93, ICICI added two new schemes to its activities. These include Agricultural Commercialisation and Enterprise (ACE) project and Trade in Environmental. Services and Technologies (TEST) programme. The ACE project, funded by the United States Agency for International Development (USAID) with a grant of US $ 20 mn, has been formulated to specifically address the critical areas of deficiency in the horticulture sector by providing financial as well as technical assistance for projects relating to post-farm activities. The TEST programme, designed to bridge technology gaps in the areas of environmental protection, is funded by USAID to the tune of US $ 25 mn and is managed by ICICI. The objective of the TEST programming is to support sustainable development through adoption of clean technologies by way of linkages between Indian and US firm.

During the year, ICICI set up a subsidiary company viz. ICICI Securities and Finance Company Ltd., (I-SEC) in association with a global financial firm J. P. Morgan and Company Inc. to offer fund and non-fund based investment banking services. ICICI's merchant banking business has been transferred to this new company. ICICI has also set up an Asset Management Company for its mutual fund. It is in the process of setting up a company to provide registrar and transfer services, entering the business of stock broking and custodial services and setting up a commercial bank.

Small Industries Development Bank of India

The Small Industries Development Bank of India (SIDBI), set up as a wholly -owned subsidiary of IDBI, is the principal financial institution for promotion, financing and development of industry in the small, tiny and cottage sectors and co-ordinating the functions of other institutions engaged in similar activities. It commenced operations on April 2, 199- on taking over IDBI's operations in respect of the small sector. SIDBI has been paying concentrated attention to the multi-dimensional growth and development of industries in the small scale sector, with special emphasis on the village, cottage and tiny sectors.

SIDBI operates various schemes of assistance comprising refinance of term loans granted by SFCs/ SIDCs/ banks and other eligible financial institutions, discounting and rediscounting of bills arising out of sale of machinery /capital equipment/ components by manufacturers in the small scale sector on deferred credit, besides rediscounting of short term trade bills arising out of sale of products of the small scale sector. SIDBI also provides equity type support to specific groups viz. women entrepreneurs, ex-servicemen, etc. Voluntary agencies, working for the development/ upliftment of under-privileged women, also are provided assistance.

SIDBI introduced two new schemes during 1992-93; equipment finance scheme for providing direct finance to existing well-run small scale units taking up technology upgradation/ modernisation and refinance for resettlement of voluntarily retired workers of NTC units, covering purchase of two or four looms or setting up of reeling units as co-operative societies. it enlarged the coverage of single window scheme (SWS), hitherto confined to new units, to include existing units in 12 identified clusters to support technology upgradation and modernisation as also provision of working capital. Also, the extent of refinance against cash credit sanctioned by banks to eligible units under SWS was raised from 50% to 75%. The limit of term loans under the automatic refinance scheme (ARS) was enhanced from Rs. 10 lakh to Rs. 50 lakh in case of scheduled commercial banks, simultaneously extending the extent of refinance from 75% to 90%, both under ARS and normal refinance scheme (NRS).

During 1992-93, SIDBI set up a venture capital fund exclusively for small scale units, with an initial corpus of Rs. 10 crore. it enrolled itself as an institutional member of the OTC Exchange of India (OTCEI).

Industrial Reconstruction Bank of India

Industrial Reconstruction Bank of India (IRBI) was set up in 1985 under the IRBI Act, 1984 on reconstitution of the erstwhile Industrial Reconstruction Corporation of India. IRBI was originally set up as the principal agency for undertaking reconstruction and rehabilitation of sick and closed industrial units. However, with the withdrawal of the Government stipulation that 60% of its portfolio should consist of sick companies, IRBI now finances all industrial projects for various products and services like other financial institutions.

IRBI provides financial assistance to industrial units by way of term loans, underwriting of equity/debentures and guarantees for loans deferred payments. It also offers financial services such as equipment leasing, hire-purchase and equipment finance. Besides, it offers services such as provision of infrastructure facilities, consultancy, managerial and merchant banking services.

SCICI Ltd.

The SCICI Ltd. was originally promoted by ICICI, together with other all-India financial institutions, as a specialised financial institution for encouraging and assisting development and investment in shipping, fishing and related industries. It was incorporated as a public limited company in December 1986. During 1992-93, SCICI embarked upon a major diversification programme to extend financial assistance to all sectors of the economy including the shipping industry. SCICI's portfolio now includes a variety of industries, such as automobiles & ancillaries, chemicals & petrochemicals, electronics & information technology, engineering, power generation & distribution, steel & steel products, textiles and food processing. However, shipping and fishing industries continue to be SCICI's priorities.

SCICI provides assistance in the form of rupee and foreign currency loans, underwriting/ direct subscriptions to shares, bonds and debentures, guarantees, deferred credit and equipment leasing. It also assists in the rehabilitation of sick but viable shipping companies and renders financial advisory and merchant banking services for raising finance, capital restructuring, etc.

Specialised Financial Institutions

A. Risk Capital and Technology Finance Corp. Ltd.

The Risk Capital and Technology finance Corporation Ltd. (RCTC) was set up in January 1988 on reconstitution of the Risk Capital Foundation (RCF) which was promoted by IFCI in 1975 to cater to the risk capital needs of the first generation entrepreneurs. RCTC provides both risk capital and venture capital assistance. Technology finance is provided for projects envisaging advancement, promotion, transfer, adaptation and commercialisation of new technologies. RCTC provides assistance in the form of conventional loans and interest-free conditional loans on a profit and risk sharing basis with the project promoters. RCTC also subscribes to the equity of projects with suitable buy-back arrangements with the promoters.

B. Technology Development and Information Company of India Ltd.

The Technology Development and Information Company of India Ltd. (TDICI) was established by ICICI and UTI under the Companies Act in July 1988 as India's first venture finance company. TDICI took over the venture capital operations of ICICI and commenced operations in August 1988. TDICI provides assistance to small and medium industries conceived by technocrat entrepreneurs including first generation entrepreneurs in the form of project loans, direct subscription to equity and a quasi-equity instrument called conditional loan. Its operations encompass venture capital funded under a UTI scheme and Development Assistance given out of DfW–IDF funds loaned by ICICI. TDICI also provides its client companies a comprehensive techno-managerial support and guidance services and works closely with research and development organisations, industry organisations, professional groups and experts in various technologies and industries. It also offers a modern technology information service.

C. Tourism Finance Corporation of India Ltd.

The Tourism Finance Corporation of India Ltd. (TFCI), promoted by IFCI together with other all India financial institutions and some nationalised banks as a public limited company under the Companies Act, 1956, is a specialised all India development financing institution for the tourism industry. It became operational on February 1, 1989.

TFCI provides financial assistance for setting up and/or development of tourism-related activities, facilities and services including hotels, restaurants, holiday resorts, amusement parks and complexes for entertainment, education and sports, safari parks, ropeways, cultural centres, convention halls, all forms of transport, air taxies, travel and tour operating agencies, tourism emporia, sports facilities, etc. TFCI provides assistance in the form of rupee loans, underwriting/direct subscription to shares/debentures, suppliers' credit, equipment leasing and equipment procurement. It provides assistance together with all-India financial institutions in respect of projects costing over Rs. 5 crore and jointly with state-level financial institutions and banks for projects costing between Rs. 1 crore and Rs. 5 crore. Projects assisted by state-level institutions and banks continue to be refinanced by IDIBI/SIDBI. Projects costing up to Rs. 1 crore are exclusively financed by TFCI.

During 1992-93, the Tourism Advisory and Financial Services Corporation of India Ltd. (TAFSIL), sponsored by TFCI to provide consultancy services in the field of tourism, became operational. TRCI became a member of OTC Exchange of India Ltd. during the year; this would help it in playing its role more effectively in mobilising resources for tourism industry. TFCI is making all efforts to augment the resources of tourism industry so as to achieve the objectives of the National Action Plan for Tourism Industry.

Life Insurance Corporation of India

The Life Insurance Corporation of India (LIC) was established under the LIC Act in 1956 after taking over life insurance business from private companies to carry on the business of life insurance and deploy the funds in accordance with the Plan priorities. LIC operates a variety of schemes so as to benefit individuals and groups from both the urban and rural areas.

As dictated by its investment policy, LIC has to invest not less than 75% of the accretions to its Controlled Fund in Central and State Government securities including Government-guaranteed marketable securities and in the socially-oriented sectors. Besides investing in Government and other approved securities. LIC provides loans for housing, rural electrification, water supply, sewerage and other socially oriented purposes. It also provides direct assistance to the corporate sector in the form of term loans and underwriting/direct subscription to shares and debentures. Besides, it extends resource support to other term lending institutions y way of subscription to their shares and bonds and also by way of term loans.

Unit Trust of India

The Unit Trust of India (UTI) was set up under an Act of Parliament in 1964. UTI plays an important role in mobilising the savings of the small investors through sale of units and channelising them into corporate investments. Over the years, it has introduced a variety of schemes to meet the needs of diverse sections of investors. After an amendment to its Act in April 1986, UTI has started extending assistance to the corporate sector by way of term loans, bills rediscounting, equipment leasing and hire-purchase facilities.

The Unit Trust of India (UTI) was established in 1964 under the Unit Trust of India Act 1963 with the main objective of mobilising household savings and channelising them for rapid industrial progress. Savings are mobilised through the sale of units and funds so raised are invested in shares and debentures of companies. The income earned from these investments is distributed to unit holders by way of dividend. The income from units works out to be higher than that declared by the UTI because of the tax exemptions from income tax upto an overall limit of Rs. 10000/- of which Rs. 3000/- is available exclusively for units. Unit holders also enjoy the benefits of easy encashability as the UTI is ready to buy back units at prices determined from time to time. The UTI has now become one of the country's most popular investment institutions and there are about 5 million unit holders, 85 per cent of them are reported to be belonging to small household sector.

The growth in sale of units was modest in the first twenty years of its operation. Beginning with Rs. 19.14 crores in 1964-65 the sale of units rose to Rs. 30.64 crores in 1973-74 and further to Rs. 330.16 crores in 1983-84. Thereafter the growth in sales has been rapid; in five years sales rose by ten-fold. This bears testimony to the confidence of the small investors in the UTI in ensuring a steady return on their investment.

In the twenty-fifth year of its operation which was celebrated this year, the UTI crossed the landmark of Rs. 10000 crores in its investible resources and achieved a new high of Rs. 3700 crores in unit sales, while adding 9.21 lakh unit holding accounts. It launched its second offshore fund and participated in setting up the first Venture Capital Fund in collaboration with ICICI to foster industrial growth.

The gross income of the UTI, which was just Rs. 1.53 crores in 1964-65 has now crossed Rs. 1600 crores. The reserves and provisions have grown to Rs. 1840 crores from a meager amount of Rs. 0.07 crores in 1964-65.

The UTI mobilises savings through the sale of units under different unit schemes and savings plans. In investing its resources, the UTI's primary concern is the profitable investment of the funds in the interest of the unit holders so as to fulfil its basic objective of ensuring the unit holder's safety and security of their capital and a regular and growing return on their units.

The UTI is primarily engaged in the purchase/sale of corporate securities in the stock market. It also provides underwriting/direct subscriptions of shares and debentures of companies. The UTI's underwriting assistance is mostly in the nature of firm commitments to invest upto the amounts underwritten. The important consideration in underwriting capital issues are the previous financial performance and management record as well as future prospects o the companies concerned. Its market operations, apart from having a stabilising influence on the stock markets, help the cause of industrial development as being a net purchaser of securities and thus releasing funds for other investment outlets including the new issues market.

Over the past few years there has been a dimensional and directional change in the activities of the UTI. It launched the India Fund, its first venture into the international market. Thereafter, the India Growth Fund was launched. Both these funds serve as unique vehicles for investors abroad to participate in the Indian capital market. While the shares of India Fund are quoted on the London Stock Exchange, those of India Growth fund are quoted on the New York Stock Exchange.

On the national front, a Mutual fund Unit Scheme was introduced under which units known as Master shares were offered for public subscription. The funds mobilised through Mastershares are invested in a basket of growth oriented equities thus giving the benefits of diversification and devoid of risk to the common investors.

In the dynamic financial environment UTI has shown considerable innovation in financial engineering and marketing. It has always taken the lead in offering new instruments to harness untapped savings. Unit Linked Insurance Plan 1971 (ULIP), Childern's Gift Growth Fund, Parents Gift and Growth Fund, Charitable and Religious Trust Scheme, Capital Gains Unit Scheme, the Monthly Income Unit Scheme series and the Growing Income Unit Scheme series are some of the different schemes introduced by the UTI to suit the needs of investors from different walks of life. As a leading investment institution it has contributed significantly towards balanced and rapid development of the capital market.

Total funds mobilised by UTI during 1992-93 through sales of units amounted to Rs. 6102 crore as against Rs. 11,685.5 crore in 1991-92. As at the end of June 1993, investible funds of UTI aggregated Rs. 38,000 crore with 29 million unit-holding accounts. Despite several adverse factors in the primary and secondary capital markets, UTI was able to introduce 12 new schemes during 1992-93. Three of the schemes viz. Rajlakshmi Unit Scheme, Bhopal Gas Victims Monthly Income Plan and Senior Citizen's Unit Plan are schemes catering to special societal needs and are open-ended. Another new open-ended Unit Scheme was tailor-made to meet special liquidity and stable income needs of large institutional investors. Besides, four equity-oriented growth schemes and four regular/deferred income schemes were also introduced.

In October 1993, UTI decided to set up a new Asset Management Company and bring its close-ended Mutual Fund schemes under its purview. It is also considering to set up separate subsidiaries to take up investment banking, stock broking, corporate advisory, investor services, etc. It is also in the process of setting up a commercial bank.

General Insurance Corporation of India

The General Insurance Corporation of India (GIC) came into being in 1973 on nationalisation of general insurance companies in the country. GIC and its four subsidiaries viz. National Insurance Company Ltd., New India Assurance Company Ltd., Oriental Fire and General Insurance Company Ltd. and United India Insurance Company Ltd. operate a number of insurance schemes to meet the diverse and emerging needs of society. As per the Insurance Act, 1938 and the Government guidelines, GIC and its subsidiaries are required to channelise 70% of annual accretions to their investible funds to socially-oriented sectors of the economy. Since 1976, GIC has been extending financial assistance to corporate sector in participation with other all-India financial institutions in the form of term loans and underwriting/direct subscription to shares/debentures of both existing and new industrial undertakings.

Export-Import Bank of India

The Export Import Bank of India (EXIM Bank) was established in 1982 by an Act of Parliament as the principal financial institution for promoting, financing and facilitating India's international trade. EXIM Bank promotes Indian exports through a variety of products and services. It has devised 24 products to meet the needs of various customer groups viz. Indian customers, overseas investors and commercial banks. The exporters can avail of pre-shipment credit, suppliers' credit, overseas investment finance, export product development loans and loans for export marketing and investment vendors development finance. It also provides term investment loans to export-oriented units. Foreign Governments and agencies are offered buyers' credit and lines of credit. EXIM Bank offers export bills rediscounting facilities, refinance of suppliers' credit, refinance of term export loans to export-oriented units and bulk import finance to commercial banks in India. EXIM Bank also participates in guarantees issued by commercial banks on behalf of Indian project exporters.

Over the years, EXIM Bank has diversified its products and services and now it offers a range of products at various stages in the export cycle viz. export product development, export production, export marketing, pre-shipment and post-shipment services covering a variety of customers. Apart from finance, EXIM Bank seeks to promote exports through information and advisory services to enable exporters to evaluate international risks, export opportunities and competitiveness. Also, EXIM bank and an institutional working group constituted by EXIM Bank evaluates and approves export bids involving deferred payments and/or issue of guarantees in respect of construction, consultancy, technology services and turn-key projects. During 1992-93, EXIM Bank introduced new products of funding exporters such as Production Equipment Finance Programme, Export Marketing Finance Programme-III and Vendor Development Programme.

State Financial Corporations

The State Financial Corporations (SFCs) are state-level development financing institutions. The main objective of SFCs is to finance and promote small and medium enterprises in their respective states for achieving balanced regional growth, catalyse investments, generate employment and widen the ownership base of industry.

There are 18 SFCs in the Country, of which 17 were set up under the SFCs' Act, 1951. The Tamil Nadu Industrial Investment Corporation ltd., established in 1949 under the Companies Act, as madras Industrial Investment Corporation, also functions as a full-fledged SFC. The financial assistance provided by SFCs to the industrial units is in the form of term loans, direct subscriptions to equity/debentures, guarantees, discounting of bills of exchange and seed/special capital. The SFCs operate a number of schemes of refinance and equity-type assistance on behalf of IDBI/SIDBI. These include schemes for artisans, special target groups like SC/ST, women, ex-servicemen, physically handicapped, etc. SFCs also grant assistance for small road transport operators, setting up hotels, tourism-related activities, hospitals and nursing homes, etc.

During the year 1992-93, IDBI issued guidelines to SFCs to adopt the prudential norms in regard to income recognition, provisioning, etc. in a phased manner. A detailed action plan prepared by IDBI covering management and organisation, operations, accounting policies and prudential norms, resource mix, recapitalisation and training needs of SFCs is under the consideration of the Government of India.

State Industrial Development Corporations

The State industrial Development Corporations (SIDCs) were set up under the companies Act, 1956, in the sixties and early seventies as wholly-owned State Government undertakings for promotion and development of medium and large industries. The SIDCs act as catalysts for industrial development and provide impetus to investment in their respective states. The assistance provided by SIDCs in the form of term loans, underwriting/direct subscription to shares/debentures and guarantees. They undertake a range of promotional activities such as preparation of feasibility reports, conducting industrial potential surveys, entrepreneurship development programmes and developing industrial areas/estates. The SIDCs are also involved in setting up of medium and large industrial projects in the joint sector/ assisted sector in collaboration with private entrepreneurs or as' wholly-owned subsidiaries. The SIDCs also act as agent for providing tax benefits under the State Governments' package scheme of incentives. Some SIDCs also offer a package of developmental services which include technical guidance, assistance in plant location and co-ordination with other many of the SIDCs are making efforts to diversify their activities to enter the field of equipment leasing, merchant banking and mutual funds.

There are 28 SIDCs in the country, 11 of them functioning also as SFCs to provide assistance to small scale sector and to act as promotional agencies. Such twin-function SIDCs are in Andaman & Nicobar, Arunachal Pradesh, Daman & Diu and Dadra & Nagar Haveli, Manipur, Meghalaya, Mizoram, Nagaland, Tripura, Goa, Pondicherry and Sikkim. Seven SIDCs are also involved in infrastructure development and other extension services for the small sector.

Technical Consultancy Organisations

The Technical Consultancy Organisations (TCOs) were established by the all-India financial institutions in the seventies and eighties in association with state-level financial/development institutions and commercial banks to cater to the consultancy needs of small and medium industries and new entrepreneurs. At present, there are 17 such TCOs operating in various states, some of them covering more than one state. Besides, Karnataka has a state-sponsored TCO viz. Technical Consultancy Services Organisation of Karnataka (TECSOK).

TCOs have been designed to provide under a single roof, a total package of consultancy services to small and medium scale industry at reasonable rates. TCOs render consultancy services to individual entrepreneurs, Government departments and agencies, various state-level developmental/ financial institutions, commercial banks and other institutions in their tasks relating to industrial development and financing. Though the initial thrust of TCOs was on pre-investment studies, over the years, they have diversified their services to include (i) preparation of project profiles and feasibility studies, (ii) undertaking industrial potential surveys, (iii) identification of potential entrepreneurs and providing them with technical and management assistance, (iv) undertaking market research and surveys for specific products, (v) undertaking energy audit and energy conservation assignments, (vi) project supervision and, where necessary, rendering technical and administrative assistance, (vii) taking up assignments on turn-key basis, (viii) undertaking export consultancy for export-oriented projects based on modern technology, (ix) offering management consultancy services, especially for diagnostic studies of sick units or for improvement in the existing units and their rehabilitation programmes, and (x) conducting Entrepreneurship Development Programmes and Skill Upgradation Programmes.

Other Institutions

A. Commercial Banks

The Scheduled Commercial Banks (SCBs) in the country comprise the State Bank of India and its associate banks (8), nationalised banks (20), private sector banks (23), regional rural banks (196) and foreign banks (24). As on March 31, 1993, the total number of branches of SCBs was 61,235, of which 35,301 (57.6% of the total) were in rural areas.

The year 1992-93 witnessed several policy initiatives relating to commercial banks which were aimed at enabling them to function in a more competitive environment. The Reserve Bank of India (RBI) liberalised many of its policies for commercial banks. The Branch Licensing Policy, which had been liberalised in April 1992 for providing adequate banking infrastructure throughout the country, was further liberalised in October 1992. Banks are now permitted to shift their existing branches within the same locality, open specialised branches for industrial finance/SSIs/NRIs/treasury, open extension counters and convert the existing rural branches into satellite offices if the existing branches are found nonviable after complying with certain minimal formalities. RBI also formulated guidelines in January 1993 for establishment of new banks in the private sector. Some of the important guidelines relate to minimum paid-up capital of Rs. 100 crore, prudential norms, capital adequacy, liquidity requirements, priority sector lending, listing in stock exchanges, use of modern infrastructural facilities, etc. In April 1992, RBI issued detailed guidelines to commercial banks with regard to asset classification, income recognition and provisioning-write-off, which are required to be achieved by them in a phased manner by 1994-95. Owing to the practical difficulties faced by the banks, some relaxations in the norms were introduced for the two accounting years ending March 31, 1993 and March 31, 1994. Despite the relaxations the new norms would adversely affect the balance sheets of banks. The Government, therefore, made a provision of Rs. 5700 crore in the 1993-94 Budget for recapitalisation of nationalised banks.

During the year under review, two committees were set up to examine the industrial credit policy as also guidelines and norms for credit delivery by the banking system. The first Committee (Chairman: Shri Rashid Jilani) constituted by the Indian Banks Association at the instance of RBI, reviewed the present cash credit system of lending followed by banks in extending working capital and the second Committee (Chairman: Shri G. V. Sheety) constituted by RBI examined the guidelines relating to lending under consortium arrangement. A number of changes were effected by RBI in the Credit Monitoring Arrangement to impart more flexibility to banks in meeting the demand for industrial credit expeditiously. Commercial banks were permitted to deviate from norms for inventory and receivables for assessing the maximum permissible bank finance. The issue of adequacy of institutional credit to the small scale industries (SSIs) was examined by the Committee on Small Scale Industrial Units (Chairman : Shri P. R. Nayak). Based on the recommendations of the Committee, RBI introduced a special package of measures for financing SSIs and advised banks to take various measures aimed at increasing the credit flow to the SSIs and arresting the problem of sickness in the SSIs. Availability of credit to the SSI sector improved further with the stipulation on foreign banks to extend at least 10% of their net bank credit to the SSI sector and to deposit the shortfall, if any, with SIDBI.

In the light of the large-scale irregularities of banks in securities transactions, RBI set up a Working Group to look into the existing inspection system and suggest a new system of inspection and supervision. The new system recommended by the Working Group comprises annual financial inspection, audit of select items by statutory auditors, management audit, etc. RBI also announced the setting up of the Board for Financial Supervision.

B Khadi and Village Industries Commission

The Khadi and Village Industries Commission (KVIC) was established in 1956 by an Act of Parliament. KVIC is engaged in the development of khadi and village industries in rural areas. Initially, besides khadi, it had under its preview, 26 village industries. After amendment to KVIC Act in July 1987, the coverage of its activities was widened and, as a result, many more new village industries were identified and brought under its fold. The KVIC's main objectives are provision of employment in rural areas, skill upgradation, transfer of technology, building up of strong rural community base and helping in rural industrialisation. The main features of the khadi and village industries under the purview of KVIC are the ability to use locally available raw materials, skills and markets, low per capital investment, simple production techniques, short gestation period and, above all, production of consumer goods. The activities of KVIC serve the underprivileged classes including scheduled castes and scheduled tribes, women, physically handicapped and minority communities in inaccessible hilly and border areas. The activities include procurement and distribution of raw materials to the producers, assistance in marketing and development and distribution of suitable tools and implements. Besides in-house research facilities, KVIC has established linkages with reputed organisations for innovating on the existing tools and equipment.

The KVIC development programmes are implemented through a network of 30 state KVI boards which are statutory organisations set up under State Legislation, 2612 institutions registered under Societies Registration Act, 1960, and 29,813 Co-operative Societies registered under State Co-operative Acts. Individuals also are assisted by KVIC through the State KVI Boards. More than two lakh villages in the country are now covered by the khadi and village industries programme.

C. National Small Industries Corporation Ltd.

The National Small Industries Corporation Ltd. (NSIC), established by the Government of India in 1955, is engaged in promoting and developing small scale industries in the country. The range of NSIC's activities includes supply of indigenous and imported machinery on easy hire-purchase and leasing terms, marketing of the products of small industries on consortia basis, export marketing of the products of small industries and assisting the development of export-worthiness of small scale units. Besides, NSIC also enlists small scale units for participation in Government stores purchase programmes, development and modernisation of prototypes of machines, equipment and tools and supply and distribution of indigenous and imported raw materials. NSIC is also engaged in training of personnel in various technical trades and co-operation with other developing countries in transfer of technology and setting up of small scale projects on turn-key basis.

D. Stock Holding Corporation of India Ltd.

The Stock Holding Corporation of India Ltd. (SHCIL) was incorporated in 1987 jointly by IDBI, IFCI, ICICI, LIC, UTI, GIC and IRBI to provide comprehensive custodial services. SHCIL has the Government mandate to act as a central securities depository in the country and to provide well developed and fully automated infrastructural facilities for trade, clearance, settlements and depository services for securities and monetary instruments. SHCIL commenced operations in August 1988. Following the Government mandate in 1991, SHCIL commenced work on setting a national clearing and depository system and proposes to introduce electronic book entry transfers.

E. State Small Industries Development Corporations

The State Small Industries Development Corporations (SSIDCs) were set up in various states under the Companies Act, 1956, as State Government undertakings to cater to the primary developmental needs of the small, tiny and village industries in the State/Union Territories under their jurisdiction. Incorporation under the Companies Act has provided SSIDCs with greater operational flexibility and wider scope for undertaking a variety of activities for the benefit of the small sector.

Some of the important activities undertaken by SSIDCs are (i) procurement and distribution of scarce raw materials, (ii) supply of machinery on hire-purchase basis, (iii) providing assistance for marketing of the products of small scale units, (iv) construction of industrial estates/sheds, providing allied infrastructure facilities and their maintenance, (v) extending seed capital assistance on behalf of the State Governments concerned and (vi) providing management assistance to production units.

In line with the changing environment, SSIDCs are changing their role from raw material distributors to organisations that will take care of various aspects of small industry development, especially marketing. This would help the tiny and small industries increase their market share. SSIDCs' assistance would help establishment of counseling and common testing facilities and provision of a mechanism to allow incorporation of the latest technology in the small sector. Some of the SSIDCs are in the process of setting up centres for display of/and information dissemination on SSI products and for providing small office spaces for SSIs in need.

Analysis/discussion that follows pertains to ten SSIDCs located in Andhra Pradesh, Assam, Goa, Bihar, Gujarat, Kerala, Maharashtra, Rajasthan, Tamil Nadu and Himachal Pradesh.

Operations of Financial Institutions

In true with the fall in inflation rate, RBI announced reduction in lending and deposits rates. Financial institutions also revised their minimum long term lending rates four times since November 1992. IDBI, for the first time, introduced from December 15, 1993, a concept of Long Term Prime Rate (LTPR) and a variable interest rate for lending at the option of the borrower. ICICI also introduced a similar scheme for offering the facility on a selective basis.

Aggregate assistance sanctioned by all financial institutions (AFIs) viz. IDBI, IFCI, ICICI, SIDBI, IRBI, SCICI, RCTC, TDICI, TFCI, LIC, UTI, GIC, SFCs and SIDCs during 1992-93 rose by

35.2% to Rs. 31,266.9 crore. Disbursements during the same period went up by 37.2% to Rs. 21,794.1 crore. Sanctions of All-India Development Banks viz. IDBI, IFCI, ICICI, SIDBI, IRBI and SCICI increased by 26.2% to Rs. 21,658.7 crore, while those of investment institutions viz. LIC, UTI and GIC recorded a rise of 66.8% to Rs. 9750.2 crore. The specialised financial institutions viz. RCTC, TDICI and TFCI sanctioned assistance aggregating Rs. 168.6 crore which was 26.6% higher then the previous year. The sanctions of SFCs at Rs. 2025.4 crore were lower by 7.5%, while those of SIDCs at Rs. 1058.8 crore were higher by 4.9%. Cumulatively, up to end-March 1993, assistance sanctioned by AFIs aggregated Rs. 1,51,522.7 crore, while disbursements amounted to Rs. 1,08,595.1 crore.

The well-integrated network of financial institutions in the country comprises 12 institutions at the national level and 46 at the state level. The structure consists of six All-India Development Banks (AIDBs), three Specialised Financial Institutions (SFIs), three Investment Institutions, 18 State Financial Corporations (SFCs) and 28 State Industrial Development Corporations (SIDCs). The AIDBs are Industrial Development Bank of India (IDBI), Industrial Finance Corporation of India Ltd. (IFCI),Industrial Credit and Investment Corporation of India Ltd. (ICICI), Small Industries Development of India (SIDBI), Industrial Reconstruction Bank of India (IRBI) and SCICI Ltd. The SFIs are Risk Capital and Technology Finance Corporation Ltd. (RCTC), Technology Development and Information Company of India Ltd. (TDICI) and Tourism Finance Corporation of India Ltd. (TFCI). The Investment institutions are Life Insurance Corporation of India (LIC), Unit Trust of India (UTI) and Genera Insurance Corporation of India (GIC). The above institutions together with SFCs and SIDCs are grouped as All Financial Institutions for the purpose of this Report.

Of the AIDBs, IDBI, IFCI, ICICI, IRBI and SCICI provide assistance to medium and large industries and SIDBI to the tiny and small industries sector. The AIDBs also undertake promotional and developmental activities. Among the SFIs, RCTC and TDICI offer risk capital, venture capital and technology development financing, and TFCI is engaged in assisting hotels, tourism and related projects. Among the investment institutions, LIC and GIC primarily take care of the life insurance and general insurance needs of the society respectively, while UTI mobilises savings of the community for channelising into productive sectors. The Investment Institutions are also active participants in assisting industry both by way of term loans and underwriting/direct subscription to equity and debentures. The SFCs provide assistance mainly to small sector and SIDCs to the medium and large sectors in their respective states. Besides, they undertake promotional and developmental activities.

The world economy has witnessed significant changes in recent years with more and more countries opening their economic frontiers and a truly global economy may emerged by turn of the century. Such prospects are very encouraging, particularly for the emerging economies such as ours. India has played an important role in the successful conclusion of Uruguay Round and can expect increasing gains from world trade and global financial system.

The policy reforms initiated in the past four years by the Government of India have had an invigorating effect on various sectors of the economy which is well poised for accelerated growth in the years to come. With a sustained revival in industrial activity and a high level of agricultural production for the seventh successive year, the Gross Domestic Product (GDP) in 1994-95 rose by 5.3% as compared with 0.9% in 1991-92 and 4.3% successively in 1992-93 and 1993-94. With a manageable trade deficit and a none-too-significant current account a gap in 1993-94 and 1994-95, substantial benefit is accruing to the

Table 2
Assistance Sanctioned and Disbursed by AFIs

(Rs. crore)

Year	Sanctions	Growth rate %	Disburse-ments	Growth rate %
1964-65	118.1	–	90.5	–
1970-75	1916.7	–	1296.7	–
1975-80	6138.0	–	4049.9	–
1980-81	2512.2	–	1603.4	–
1981-82	2723.6	8.4	2065.6	28.8
1982-83	3218.4	18.2	2371.9	14.8
1983-84	4087.1	27.0	2936.4	23.8
1984-85	5546.4	35.7	3502.6	19.3
1985-86	6368.8	14.8	4925.9	40.6
1986-87	7880.2	23.7	5656.0	14.8
1987-88	8846.2	12.3	6670.1	17.9
1988-89	13566.7	53.4	9064.5	35.9
1989-90	14637.3	7.9	9603.5	5.9
1990-91	18432.1	25.9	11775.4	22.6
1991-92	23118.7	25.4	15889.0	34.9
1992-93	32166.9	35.2	21794.1	37.2
Cummulative up to end-March 1993	151522.7		108595.1	

economy out of the growth in GDP. With the corporate sector also reporting excellent results and with favourable development on the agricultural front, the growth in GDP is projected to rise by 6% in 1995-96.

The process of economic reforms has imparted a new dynamism to the domestic industry as well. There is a growing recognition about the need for the Indian industry to seize the opportunities to face global competition. It is heartening to note that domestic industry has already demonstrated resilience and capability to withstand international competition. Many companies are in the process of restructuring their operations by evaluating their strengths and weaknesses and identifying the niches by forging strategic alliance with other firms, both domestic and international. The privatisation process has also opened up avenues for massive investments in sectors such as power, infrastructure and tele-communication. Indian corporates have responded positively in perceiving these emerging avenues for growth and have come forward to set up mega project. This called for a shift in the pattern of project financing by your Company. This is apparent from the fact that the percentage share of sanctions in 1994-95 in relation to cumulative sanctions upto 31st March 1994 has gone up in basic industries group to 47.8% against 38.4% earlier with specific rises in respect of Power Generation at 18.8% against 5.3%. Petroleum Refinery at 7.5% against 2.9% and for Shipping and Construction industry at 2.1% against 0.2%. Business prospects for your Company are bright, more so since many such mega infrastructure projects and other industrial projects are expected to materialise in the near future. However, the tight money policy coupled with continuing depressed conditions in capital market and tapering FII in-flows have tended to increase the demand for debt financing leading to rising interest costs which are bound to have an impact on the profitability of corporate sector. In this context, the issue relating to securitisation of debt assume greater importance and should be seriously addressed to with a view to creating healthy secondary market for debt instruments.

Anticipating growing competition from national and international financial institutions, it has become an issue of urgent importance for development banks should set-up study group which can advice them on various areas which include Business Strategy Review, Organisational Restructuring. Human Resource Development/ Management and Operational Process. It is expected that such studies would help these banks in reorienting its business strategy and in improving the capability to record a sustained growth in future years and attain a pre-eminent position in the meantime, certain innovative measures have been introduced by these institutions with a view to ensuring that the various needs and requirements of the clients are attended to with promptitude and despatch as a result of which the response time for according approval in principle to the requests for financial assistance and final sanctions, have been curtailed drastically, with greater degree of transparency in these as well as other decision. The industry has responded well to the changing environment in and as a result, the number of proposals received by Indian Development Banks have increased manifold. In the wake of growing investment prospects in newer and non-traditional industries, these banks high degree of technical competence so as not only to ensure quality appraisal/ assessment of the projects but also serve as a source of authentic endorsement of the feasibility of the projects undertaken by the sponsors and towards this end, Indian Development Banks have started the process of developing a panel of eminent experts from diverse fields, whose experience could be drawn upon.

In the fast changing national and global economic scenario, information technology coupled with communication revolution is playing a major role in empowering the managers with timely information essential for the success and survival of an organisation. Indian Development Banks have benefits of information technology. State-of-the-art computer systems in a Local Area Network (LAN) environment are being installed. Database of business information generated from within the organisation and collected from environment are being created to strengthen the decision support systems and to meet the challenges arising out of growing competition. All the offices of development banks have been connected through National Information Centre's Satellite based network NIC-NET to avail E-Mail and Data File Transfer facilities.

Over the years, these banks had identified several gaps in the institutional infrastructure in the country and promoted various specialised institutions besides being co-promoter of various other organisations. India's financial services sector has entered a phase of structural reforms that promises the emergence of an efficient, competitive and well diversified system, capable of meeting the demands of a growing free market economy. Resultantly, in the fiercely competitive financial market place, where customer retention and complementality of service have become key factors for survival, expansion through associated diversification has become a matter of necessity as a pre-requisite to becoming a conglomerate of financial super market. Major players like have to provide the whole gamut of financial services in order to remain competitive. These banks are focusing on enlarging the network of institutions that can provide it a strategic edge in the redefined market place which is increasingly becoming global.

The various economic reforms has also witnessed sizeable growth in capital markets. With the volume and amount of transactions going up substantially in the past few years. The tremendous support in the business of capital markets has rendered the existing systems incapable of handling large volumes, introducing serious inefficiencies and delays. It has become necessary to replace the present system by a new and modern depository system, so as to eliminate paper work facilitate electronic book-entry of the transfer of securities, permit automatic and transparent screen based trading in securities, curtail settlement periods and improve liquidity. Legislation for establishment of Depositories is being contemplated by the Govt. of India. A complementary area in developing the required infrastructure for capital markets is the establishment of Clearing House (on the lines of the system operating amongst banks in respect of cheques/drafts etc.) which could settle and guarantee various transactions in the Stock Exchanges. With a view to completing the linkages in providing the range of financial services.

Concluding Observations— To conclude, the prospects for future growth in operations of Development Banks in India are quite bright. Those who are entrusted with policy framing of Development Banks are fully alive to the fundamental changes that are taking place in our operating environment. The management of these Banks have kept fine-tuned to environmental changes alongwith emergence of increasingly sophisticated client needs. Even services of these Development Banks are getting diversified, theirselves continue to emphasis stringent and internationally comparable asset quality and capital adequacy standards. Simultaneously, the Bank would actively address its agenda of expanding its client base and developing new and improved services. In the coming years and the same will would also continue to stress upon further streamlining of systems and procedures to improve credit delivery and debt recovery. These Banks would also keep up with its innovations in structuring of debt instruments so that they appropriately reflect investor preferences and strengthen the Bank's risk management capabilities.

In fine, their strategic initiatives in the future have been appositely designed so that these Banks continues to retain its premier status in the emerging configuration of institutional finance.

9

Venture Capital – A New Dimension of Financial Market in India

Nalini Prava Tripathy

The Indian Capital Market have been undergoing various changes and emerged as a major source of finance for the corporate sector. Several new Institution have appeared in the financial scenc and venture capital company have joined to expand the range of financial services. Venture capital financing is needed to augment the India's technical progress. The present paper briefly discus the concept, importance of venture capital and give some suggestion for tapping full potential of venture capital in India.

Introduction

"Whenever we see a successful business, someone once made a courageous decision. Long Range planning does not deal with future decisions but with the future of present decisions" *Peter F. Drucker.*

The Government of India implemented the economic reforms programme including financial sector reforms with the object of improve the efficiency and effectiveness of the financial system conceeding operational freedom for flexibility to it through prudential regulation and supervision in a free financial environment. And most of the financial sector reforms cover the capital market. The scenario in the Indian Capital market has changed very fast over the past decade or so. It has emerged as a major source of finance for the corporate sector savers have got attracted by the higher yield on new instrument. The Bank have come under the pressure and looking for new avenues of growth. Several institution and new instruments appeared both in capital and money market. Mutual funds have established as an important financial intermediation. Leasing, hire purchase companies and factoring services have entered into activities. New risky lines of business need support in the form of venture capital and venture capital is emerged to fill the particular need and carving out market.

Origin

The origin of venture capital is traced from USA in 19th and 20th centuries. In 1946, the American Research and Development was formed as the first venture organisation which financed over 100 companies and made over 35 times its investments. In 1989, the venture capital company provided Rs. 3,700 crores to 1500 companies. Bank also invested equivalent over 1500 crores in 1988-89. Since then venture capital is one of the important contributor in the economic development of USA, UK, Europe and Japan. The real development of venture capital took place in 1958 when the Business Administration Act was passed by the US Congress, Venture capital also achieved success in Britain due to Government's Business Expansion scheme which permitted individuals to claim tax relieves for investment in companies not listed on the stock exchanges. In UK., the concept became popular in late sixties. Japan is tempted by America to adopt the concept and new experiencing an entrepreneurial and venture capital boom. In USA venture capital created billion dollar product through digital equipment corporation, Apple Computer and silican valley. Seeing the benetils of the Western Countries which they obtain from venture capital market. India has also tempted to establish venture capital. Since then the concept of venture capital is gradually coming into vogue and the financial institution public sector banks and private sector have formed units to enter this field.

Concept of Venture Capital

The term venture capital comprises of two words viz., 'venture' and 'capital'. The dictionary meaning of venture is a course of proceeding, the outcome of which is uncertain but which is attended by the risk of danger of 'loss' and capital means resources to start the enterprise. However the term venture capital is understood in two ways. According to narrow sense the capital which is available for financing the new business ventures are called venture capital. Generally it involves finance to the growing companies. In the broad sense venture caitalis the investment of long-term equity finance where the venture caitalist earns his returns primarily in the form of capital gain. It is under the assumption that the entrepreneur and the venture capital would act as partners. It is a commitment of capital for the formation and setting up of small-scale enterprises specializing in new ides or new technologies. Venture capital does not financing to the enterprise who is engaged in trading, broking, investment or financial services, agency or liaison work. It is generally considered a high risk capital. Venture capital in the sense is not an injection of funds into new firm but also an input of the skills needed to set the firm up, design its marketing strategy, organise and mange it.

Dimension of Venture Capital

Venture capital in India is available in three forms equity, conditional loans and income notes. All venture capital funds in India provide equity, however, generally their contribution does not exceed 49 percent of the total equity capital under which the ownership of the firm remains with the entrepreneur. A conditional loan is repayable in the form of royalty ranging between 2 and 15 percent after the venture is able to generate sales and no interest is paid on such loans. The third one is income note, which has a combining feature of conventional and conditional loans and the entrepreneur has to pay both interest and royalty on sales at low rates. Venture capital investors are interested in investing at three stages in a company's development-start up, money to finance launching of an enterprise and 'growth capital' for major expansion of the company. Among the three stages, the first stage is the riskiest type of investment but assured gain. During the second stage, the venture capital groups provide finance to the entrepreneurs to carry the company to a size where it can secure capital and loans from various sources. Finally at the growth stage, venture capital helps for major expansion of the company to obtain an economy of scale.

Importance of Venture Capital

Venture capital is popular in different parts of the country as it plays a significant role in fostering industrial development by exploiting vast and untapped potentialities. It is growing due to the following importance : –

(1) Even if the entrepreneur having a good project idea but no previous entrepreneurial track record to leverage the firm, handle customers and bankers, so in this situation venture capital can help to the entrepreneurs to launch their project successfully.

(2) The rapid growth of international technology led to the growth of technology in India but indigenous technology has been slack due to unwilling of the people to take entrepreneurial risk. Thus in this situation, venture capital is assumed significant as it provide strong impetus for entrepreneurs to develop the product with the new technology and commercialise them.

(3) Venture Capital has gain its importance as it solve the problems of sickness of company.

(4) As the venture capitalists are ready to lend their expertise and standing to the entrepreneur, the local group and multinational company can easily be enter into joint venture.

(5) Venture Capitalists are also help to a large number of smaller units under which they are able to up grade their technology to meet the demands of the major industrial units.

(6) Venture Capitalists are also playing a significant role in tapping the potentiality of service sector. Thus venture capital is

booming to entrepreneurs to exploit the potential of Indian economy. All this will go along way in broadening the industrial base, creation of jobs flushing of exports and overall enrichment of the economy.

Venture Capital in India

The Finance Minister in 1988–89 felt the difficulties of the new entrepreneur to raise equity capital hence he announced to formulate a scheme under which venture capital companies or funds will be enabled to invest in new companies and be eligible for concessional treatment of capital gains available to new corporate entities. Thus, venture capital financing has come to assume significance to develop entrepreneurship and exploit technological potential in India. Though venture capital is of very recent origin in India, there are a few schemes prevalent for financing of this kind.

1. Risk Capital and Technology Finance Corporation Limited.

The Risk Capital and Technology Finance corporation limited (RCTC) was set up in January 1988 on reconstitution of the Risk Capital foundation which was promoted by IFCI in 1975 to cater to the risk capital needs of the first generation entrepreneurs. RCTC provides both risk capital and venture capital assistance. It has an authorised capital of Rs. 25 crores and a paid up capital of Rs. 50 crores. RCTC provides assistance in the form of conventional loans and interest-free conditional loans on a profit and risk sharing basic with the project promoters. During 1992-93 RCTC sanctioned assistance aggregating Rs. 15 crore and disbursed a sum of Rs. 10.4 crore recording a growth of 35.1% in sanctions and 23.8 percent in disbursement over the previous year. Assistance sanctioned under venture capital scheme–III increased by 61.3% to Rs. 10 crore and constituted 66.7 percent of total sanctions. Sanctions under risk capital scheme increased by 56.7 percent to Rs. 4.7 crore in 1992-93 while those under technology finance scheme fell from Rs. 1.9 crore in 1991-92 to Rs. 0.3 crores in 1992-93, cumulatively RCTC sanctioned assistance aggregating Rs. 64.9 crore and disbursed a sum of Rs. 48.5 crore.

2. Venture Capital Fund

The Government of India enacted Research and Development Act 1986 imposing levy and collection of tax of 5% on all payment made for import of Technology. The fund is collected to provide financial assistance to those industrial concerns who adopt imported technology to widen domestic application. The venture capital fund was set up by long term fiscal policy of the Government with an initial capital of Rs. 10 crores to provide equity capital or pilot plants. However this scheme came into effect from the later half of 1987. Under this scheme equity fund is disbursed with out any interest and voting rights. The minimum and maximum project assistenc ranges between Rs. 5 and 250 lacs. The assistence veries from 85 to 90 percent of the project cost.

3. Technology Development and Information Co. of India Limited (TDICI)

The Technology Development and Intermation Company of India Limited (TDICI) was established by ICICI and UTI under the companies act in July 1988 as India's first venture finance company. TDICI took over the venture capital operations of ICICI and commenced operation in August 1988. It started with an authorised capital of Rs. 20 crores which was to be increased to Rs. 40 to 50 crores. TDICI provide assistance to small and medium industries which was setup by technocrat entrepreneurs in the form of equity conditional loans and convertible debenture. It also offers a modern technology information service. TDICI has managed the first venture fund of Rs. 20 crores subscribed equally by ICICI and UTI. This is the first fund floated to provide venture capital to entrepreneurs in the country and is a part of venture capital unit scheme, an innovative scheme of UTI. In January 1990, ICICI and UTI have jointly launched their second venture take for Rs. 100 crores. The aggregate assistence sanctioned by TDICI during 1992–93 rose by 53.8% to Rs. 28.6 crores. Direct subscription to equity accounted for bulk 69.6 percent of the sanctions. Assistance disbursed during the year also went up by 30.3 percent to Rs. 23.2

crore on a cumulative basis, up to end-march 1993, sanctions aggregated Rs. 81.2 crores and disbursements amounted to Rs. 66.1 crores.

(4) Indus Venture Capital Funds

Indus venture capital fund is one of the private venture capital fund which have been established in India. It has been established with a capital of Rs. 2 crore contributed by several Indian and International institutions and companies. The investment of the fund will be managed by a separate company, Indus venture management limited. The company will provide both equity capital as well as management support to entrepreneur International finance corporation recently invested $ .50 million to help establish privately managed venture capital fund. Indus venture management limited will be owned to the extent of 35 percent by the private sector, 30 percent by internationals and 35 by the Government of India. However it will not invest more than 10 percent of its fund in one project and will take up to 50 percent of the project equity. The main aim is to seek long-term capital gains through equity investment high-risk, high return investments in private companies.

(5) Gujrat Venture Finance Limited

GVFI Gujrat venture finance limited was promoted by the Gujrat Industrial Investment Corporation (GIIC) Limited in July, 1990, to provide venture finance. The total size of the fund is Rs. 24 crores contributed by GIIC, IDBI, the World Bank, Commercial Banks, SFCS and Private Corporate bodies. The extent of financing ranges between Rs. 2.5 lakh and Rs. 2 crores GVFI provides venture financial assistance in the form of equity and quasi-equity instruments. It provides management support to entrepreneurs.

(6) Credit Capital Venture Fund

Credit Capital Venture fund is the first private managed venture capital fund set up in April 1989 with Rs. 10 crores to be subscribed by International Financial agencies to the extent of Rs. 6.5 crores and the remaining through public subscription.

(7) State Bank, Canara Bank and Grindays Bank Venture Capital Funds

SBI's merchant Banking subsidiary, SBI capital market (SBI cap) setup of VC fund for brought out deals. SBI cap invests in the equity shares of new and unknown companies. Can bank also setup venture capital fund through its can bank financial services. Grindlays bank has started venture capital fund and it provides venture capital assistence to high risk projects.

Suggestions and Conclusion

Venture capital finance is an instrument inducing technological development stimulating creativity and innovation and nurturing entrepreneurship. Thus efforts are required by the Government, financial institutions, private sector and other agencies to create environment for the growth of venture capital in India. The following are for of suggestion for developing venture capital market :

(1) To promote and develop venture capital business the Union Government should give fiscal reliefs in the shape of excepting returns from capital gains tax and modify stock market regulations to provide quick exit routes.

(2) The Government should provide long-term finance for venture capital companies through public financial institutions establish an unlisted security market and encourage stock option scheme as an incentive for venture capitalists.

(3) There is poor awareness about the availability of venture capital finance from private and public sector institutions. There is no direct advertisement/publicity. This should be corrected.

(4) Venture capital finance involves risk but high risk involves high returns both for entrepreneur and financiers. If this is accepted as reality there will be better market.

(5) Generally public sector institutions look for return on capital rather than capital appreciation. There is need for a change in out look.

(6) An entrepreneurial tradition must be more broad-based and less family-based. This calls for imparting education and training in entrepreneurship.

(7) Debt/Equity gearing of 1.5:1 is unsealisticit will be difficult for the promoter to meet this requirement of the venture capital companies. It should be at least 3:1.

(8) Tax concessions should be given to banks for setting up venture capital fund through subsidiaries so that the companies can seek venture capital assistances.

Lastly orderly and efficient mechanisms must be evolved to facilitate liquidation of investments of venture capital funds.

Conclusion

To sum up, venture capital facilitates a large number of technological opportunities for the creation and commercialisation of new goods and services. Thus the concept will certain meet India's need in science, industry and economy but all in all venture capital scenario in India would bright depending upon the implementation of suggestions.

References

1. Mishra, Asimk, "Venture Capital Financing : Concept and Indian Scenario", *Finance India* Vol VII No. 1 March 1993.
2. Fatnam, B, Venture Capital & its Indian Scenario, *Vichar vol–5*, April 1992.
3. Gupta, Snehlata," Venture Capital in India", *Business Analys,* Volume 14, July-December 1993.

4. Manohar, R., "Venture Capital – An analysis". *Financial Express* 15 March 1988.

5. *Business India,* January 22-February 4, 1990.

6. Chandra, Prasanna., *Financial Management,* Tata Mc Graw-Hill Publishing Company Limited, New Delhi.

7. Srivastava, R. M., *Management of Indian Financial Institutions,* Himalaya Publishing House, Bombay.

8. Pandey, I. M. "Venture Capital – the adventure" *Chartered financial Analyst,* July 1994.

Over The Counter Exchange of India (OTCEI)

.Mayura Pandya

The fillip given by the 1985-86 boom to the Indian financial sector has resulted in the emergence of plethora of services : equipment leasing, hire-purchase, consumer durables financing, real-estate financing and non-fund based financial services like stock market activities, bill discounting, factoring, merchant banking and allied activities, setting a respectable pace of growth which, if sustained, may turn Bombay into a leading centre of the international financial market.

As a consequence of the rapid potential growth in capital market services, several new agencies and institutions have emerged notably, Securities and Exchange Board of India (SEBI), Stock Holding Corporation of India (SHCIL), Credit Rating & Information Services (I) Ltd. (CRISIL) and Discount & Finance House of India (DFHIL). The latest entrant to the financial arena is the OTCEI – Over The Counter Exchange of India – India's first unlisted security market which is expected to give the financial sector a new dimension.

Background

Over The Counter (OTC) business is not an innovation of Indian financial wizards. It is just another idea adopted from the major financial centres of the world such as the Tokyo OTC market. The London Unlisted Securities Market (USM) and the American National Association of Security Dealers Automated Quotations (NASDAQ).

In India, the peculiar events in the growth of the stock markets were largely responsible for creating the environment that made an OTC exchange the need of the hour. The shortage of floating stock of good scrips in the market coupled with growing mutual fund operations and the consequent artificial scarcities created by bull operators skyrocketed prices to astronomical levels. The bullish trend was further accentuated by the off-shore funds, their ultimate destinations being equities. It was a case of poverty (of scrips) in the midst of plenty (of investible funds).

At this point, the only possible alternative for investors seemed to be the equities of lesser known and new companies. However, investors were hesitant to venture into this area largely for two reasons: Investor confidence had taken a severe jolt in the 1985-86 boom when lesser known and new (fly-by-night) companies had vanished with public funds; and the rigid listing requirements of Indian bourses which kept low-equity but viable companies, the outlet was also needed for the new venture capital projects of Rs. 3 crores and less being promoted by TDICI and others which were facing listing problems on the major stock exchanges.

In the backdrop of these events, the working group in its report submitted in 1989 had among others suggested the creation of a multi tier system of listing securities which would categories companies into two or more tires wherein each tier would list scrips having some similarity in their attributes. This multi-tier system is expected to replace the existing one.

While the report called on the Securities and Exchange Board of India (SEBI) to prepare a workable model, ICICI took the cue with UTI in January, 1990 to put up the proposal as the main promoters of the OTC company. Accordingly, they submitted an application to the Registrar of Companies for setting up an OTC company along with a few other financial institutions. Several modalities have since been finalised and the proposal awaits final clearance from the government.

The Exchange

The OTCEI has been incorporated as a company under Section 25 of the Indian Companies Act, 1956. While the ultimate OTC Exchange will be a ringless, electronically traded, automated national market, it is intended to set it up in stages. Initially, trading will be conducted in a manual mode, namely, through personal communication, operating only within Bombay. Progressively, electronic trading will be introduced and other centres linked. The exchange will be non-profit making and free of income-tax liability. This carries with it the obligation that the gains from the business should be ploughed back into the operations. There will be no dividend payments. It has been promoted by UTI, ICICI, IDBI, IFCI, LIC, GIC, SBI Capital Markets Ltd., and Canbank Financial Service Ltd.

Management

The Board of Directors of the OTC Exchange are professionals from the promoting institutions. Dr. S. A. Dave, the then Chairman of UTI is the Chairman of the OTC Exchange while Mr. Ravi Mohan from Merchant Banking Division of ICICI is to be the Chief Executive.

The Corporate office of the OTCEI is situated at 117, Market Chambers III, Nariman Point, Bombay 400021 while the Registered office is at 13, Sir Vithaldas Thackersay Marg, New Marine Lines, Bombay - 400020.

Capital Structure

The total capital of the OTCEI is Rs. 5.0 crores contributed to the various promoters mentioned earlier. The share of each promoters is under 20 per cent each by UTI and ICICI, 17 per cent by IDBI, 11 per cent by SBI CAP and 8 per cent each by the remaining participants.

Objectives

The objective of the OTC of India is two-fold: (i) To create a stock exchange which will help companies raise finance from the capital market in a cost effective manner, and (ii) To provide a facile and efficient channel of capital market investment for the growing investor community.

More than ever, today the increasing investor populace which is estimated at over 15 million needs to be protected and encouraged to contribute to nation building investment. Rather, the lack of a fool-proof system, strict ethical codes and accountable regulatory mechanism have caused investors to face problems of liquidity, inaccessibility, delayed settlements and transfers to mention a few. Moreover, the greenhorn investor usually finds the subtle nuances of the stock market game abstruse. As a result he is often unaware to the actual price at which the transaction took place on his behalf.

Besides the investor community, yet another segment of the economy known as the "under Rs. 3 crores segment" has been facing problems. From a sample of 200 companies which were in existence for at least 5 years, selected from as many as 15 industries, it was noted in a study of new issues by SEBI that these issues were mainly made by small and medium-sized companies which were vulnerable in terms of profitability and encountered difficulties in both raising resources at the same cost as large companies and in providing adequate liquidity to the scrips.

Benefits

The benefits of the OTC Exchange will accrue mainly to the companies and the investor besides the economy in general. It provides a method of raising funds for companies through capital market instruments which are priced fairly. In OTCEI the company will be able to negotiate the issue price of its shares of the company with the sponsors who will market the issue. It will save unnecessary issue expenses on raising funds from capital markets. The method of sponsors placing the scrips with members of the OTCEI who will in turn off-load the scrips to the public will obviate the need for a public issue. As a result all associated costs will be eliminated. It will retain greater degree of management stability. The OTCEI will list scrips even with 20% of the capital made available to the public.

Further it provides greater accessibility to large pool of captive investor base, enhancing fund raising power substantially. OTCEI will create a nationwide network where investors who form the captive investor base for companies will be serviced. It will help project a better image of the company. The sound market standing of the sponsor lends credibility to the company's image making its securities more acceptable to investors. Moreover, all the companies listed on the OTC market will get the status of a public limited company which will help them reduce their tax pany is 40 per cent plus surcharge whereas for private limited companies engaged in manufacturing, the tax is 45 per cent plus surcharge and those engaged in trading 50 per cent plus surcharge. Thus, the tax advantage to private companies engaged in trading works out to a high as 10 per cent which is quite attractive.

The new arrangement will also benefit investors. First of all investment in stocks will become easier. OTCEI's wide network will make the stock exchange easily accessible to the investor. It will provide greater confidence and fidelity of trade. Investor can look up the prices displayed at each OTC counter. He knows he is trading in the scrips at the right market price. It also enables transactions to be completed quickly. Investors can settle the deals across the counter and the money or scrip proceeds from the deal will be settled in a matter of days. Additionally it will provide definite liquidity to investors. The market making system proposed to be introduced in the OTCEI will have two-way prices which are quoted regularly to provide sufficient opportunity for investors to exit. Besides investor may get a greater sense of security because all scrips have been researched and members have been willing themselves to invest in these scrips.

OTCEI will help spread the stock exchange operations geographically and integrate capital market investment into a national forum. It will besides encouraging closely-held companies to go public, promote venture capital activities to boost entrepreneurship. It will give a boost to the growth of finance companies by providing a hitherto untapped area of operation and therefore a new source of profit. It will promote the growing cadre of finance professionals yet another area of specialisation. And, finally, it will contribute to the conducive environment needed to attract foreign funds, particularly NRI funds, to new ventures.

Market Constituents

The major market constituents of the OTCEI will be: (a) Companies; (b) Investors; (c) Members; (d) Licensed Dealers.

Companies : The following types of companies are expected to seek listing on the OTCEI.

(i) Companies with equity capital of less than Rs. 3 crores and /or making a public offer of less than Rs. 1.8 crores. (ii) Closely held companies wanting to go public. (iii) Companies assisted by venture capitalists. (iv) Regular companies seeking funds from capital markets, and (v) Unlisted companies.

Investors : While the existing investor base will form the target market for OTCEI, it is expected that more serious, conservative and long term investors would prefer OTCEI. This is because the price variations are expected to be more controlled in the OTCEI and are not likely to spurt and crash in the manner it happens in the regular stock exchanges. The investor base would naturally expand as new OTC counters are set up.

Members and Licensed Dealers : Members and licensed dealers will both 'make market' in scrips listed on OTCEI i.e. they will trade/deal in all scrips. (Market making means quoting two-way prices at which the licensed dealer/member is willing to buy or sell or sell a standard quantity of scrips which will be continuously quoted). The difference between members and licensed dealers is that the members can also act as sponsors to listing of new scrips.

Sponsorship role includes following functions : (i) Appraise the project and company (including management, market viability, technical, commercial, economic, environment and government clearance aspects). (ii) Value the scrip to be listed on the OTCEI. (iii) Sponsor the scrip to other members and licensed dealers and place the entire scrips (to be offered to public subsequently) with them. (iv) Make market for at least three years from the date the scrips are offered for public trading compulsorily. (v) Arrange for at least one more member/licensed dealer to make market in the scrip for at least one year from the date of public offer compulsorily.

All other members and dealers are eligible to make market voluntarily. Voluntary market making could be for limited periods of 3 months or such other longer periods as may be decided by the member/licensed dealer. The OTCEI will from time to time make such rules regarding market making as are necessary to ensure a disciplined market behaviour and its smooth operations.

Procedure of Listing Scrips on the OTCEI

The OTCEI has provided guidelines/procedure for listing of scrips on the exchange. Initially, various members of the exchange make offers to the company which after evaluating these offer appoints one of them as the sponsor. The preliminary listing requirements such as project appraisal, price fixation and other relevant terms and condition are then pursued by the sponsor. The price and the terms are usually the outcome of negotiations between the company and the sponsor. Next, the sponsor pilots the scrip placement with other

OTCEI members & licensed dealers. He also must necessarily appoint another member dealer to become a compulsory market maker in the scrip for a last one year from commencement of public trading. Failing to appoint such market maker will lead to a rejection of the listing by the OTCEI.

After the sponsor finalises the list of initial allottes who will hold the shares of the company, the company approaches the Controller of Capital Issues for permission to make the issue on the pattern suggested by the sponsor.

After obtaining the consent the company and its sponsors approach the OTCEI for a listing along with the requisite documents. On receipt of the application and the supporting documents, the OTCEI's consent to make the initial public offer is issued to the company. Subsequently, the necessary advertisements are issued and copies of prospectus and application forms are made available to the public at the counters of the appropriate members and licensed dealers. On completion of the period offer of issue, the allotment will be made on the pattern prescribed by the OTCEI and a final list prepared and funds appropriated accordingly. A detailed list of allotees and refundees is then submitted by the company to the OTCEI which approves the listing thus paving the ground for trading in the scrip.

Trading Mechanism

When a scrip is bought at an OTC, a Counter Receipt (CR) is issued which will contain details such as name of investor, name of company whose shares were sold by the counter, number of shares bought, the purchase price etc. Four copies of the CR which certifies the transaction as valid will be simultaneously prepared – one for the investor, one for the counter, one for OTCEI and one for the Registrar. The CR is issued only after the buyers's signature is obtained on the transfer deed which has the seller's signature & details duly witnessed. At the end of the day all transfer deeds along with the relevant CRs are sent to the custodian/registrar who are appointed by the OTCEI. The counter will not accept share certificates itself during transactions but will use them only as security. When the investor wants to sell, he will have to surrender the share certificate to the custodian in return for the CR.

OTCEI proposes to compile a manual of all OTC counters alongwith the name and signature of the representative authorised to deal on the OTC Exchange. Such a manual will be circulated to all the members/licensed dealers. Also a book containing updated codes assigned to each counter and their validity dates will be circulated to investors/licensed dealers, periodically.

When an investor comes to a couture to sell, he produces the CR. The CR particulars of the counters which sold to the investor, such as its code, name and signature of the authorised representative will be checked by the counter against the manual and book circulated by the OTCEI. When it matches, the deal is put through and the investor is given a cheque payable to the bank account number contained in the CR. The seller is asked to fill up the transfer deed which is taken by the counter before giving the cheque to the investor. The counter will fill up its own particulars and compete the transfer deed (TD). Along with the cheque the counter will issue a sale confirmation slip (SCS) to the investor, four copies of which are distributed, one each to the investor, the counter, the OTCEI and the custodian/registrar. At the end of the day all the TDs and the relevant SCS will be sent to the custodian for updating.

At the end of each day, copies of all the CRs and SCSs issued by each counter, along with a consolidated statement showing company-wise transactions will be sent by each counter to OTCEI. Similarly, the sponsor/company will have a contract with the custodian/registrar to provide them with an updated list of shareholders as per mutual agreement.

The counters may wish to retain the TDs filled in by sellers and transfer the scrips in their name. When the scrips are sold back, at that time, the buyer's particulars would be directly filled up and sent to the custodian/registrar for updating.

The maximum period for keeping such registered transfers will be seven days from the date of transaction, after which the counter would have to send the transfer deed to the custodian/registrar. In such an event, the counter will send the copy of the relevant SCS also along with the TDs to the custodian/registrar after seven days. But the copy of the SCS should be sent to OTCEI on the same day of the transaction. If any scrips were sold back then the TD (with the new investor's particulars as the purchaser) along with the copy of SCS and the CR (when the scrip was sold to a new investor) will be sent to the custodian/registrar.

The CR will be for the full number of shares purchased by the investor. If the investor wants to sell only part of the holding, then the CR will be exchanged for a new CR (with the reduced holding details) and an SCS for the number of shares actually sold. The new CR will carry the particulars of the counter currently doing the deal but continue to carry the original prices details.

The custodian/registrar will issue a consolidated statement to each counter once in a week to confirm that the CRs accepted by the counter were valid, after checking its records of CR issued by various counters. The counters can then destroy the CRs collected by them.

The procedure enumerated above is for transactions involving less then a 1000 shares. In case of higher number of shares, the counter will send the TD to company for endorsement. Any transactions involving more than 900 shares will be reported on the same day to the company.

It is intended to explore the possibility of merging the TD/CR/SCS into a self contained document till which time the above system will be followed.

Admission Criteria

The OTCEI has laid down certain criteria for admitting members, licensed dealers and companies into the OTC Exchange.

Members

The member should possess necessary skill, resources and capabilities to appraise projects, establish its viability, analyse company's financial worth, and evaluate company's management, determine market for company's product and ensure that the project meets with governmental regulations. The member should have necessary standing and status to be able to carry the confidence of other members and licensed dealers while recommending the scrips for investment.

The members should have enough, financial resources to be able to carry on activities of sponsorship and trading which will involve (a) ability to invest in and hold to scrips for long period, and (b) provide market making services for extended period. The members would be public financial institutions, scheduled banks, merchant banks, mutual funds and venture capital funds approved by SEBI and other non-banking financial institutions as defined by RBI directives, having a minimum tangible net worth of an amount specified by the OTCEI governing body from time to time.

The member should have adequate organisational infrastructure to carry on the following functions: (a) appraisal of project; (b) Investment; (c) OTC counter management to deal with investment; and (d) trading and market making.

Fees payable by members include a one time non-refundable admission fee of Rs. 10 lacs (Rs. 5 lacs payable immediately and Rs. 6 lacs payable after one year) plus an annual subscription fee of Rs. 1 lac.

Licensed Dealers

The licensed dealers would be a corporate body, partnership firms and individuals having minimum tangible net worth of an amount to be decided by the OTCEI from time to time. At least 40% of the share capital of such corporate bodies should be held by the promoters which holding cannot be sold without prior permission of the OTCEI.

In case of individuals, proof of having tangible net worth of an amount to be decided by the OTCEI governing body and suitable references should be furnished. The individual should be at least a graduate.

Licensed dealers are to have adequate financial strength to be able to carry on the trading and market making function. The net business exposure on OTCEI will be limited as a percentage of the net worth which is committed to OTC Exchange operation.

Licensed dealers are to have adequate knowledge of trading, stock valuation, share transfer rules and laws relating to the above. Licensed dealers are to have adequate infrastructure to carry on : (a) investment (b) trading and market making; and (c) OTC counter management. They are to be selected after an interview by the OTC committee. Fees payable by licensed dealers included a one time non-refundable admission fee of Rs. 2 lacs plus an annual subscription fee of Rs. 5000/-.

Companies

The company should be sponsored by a member of the OTCEI which will certify that it has appraised the company and its project and has found the scrips proposed to be listed on the OTC Exchange to be investment worthy. Further, the sponsor has to certify that all the scrips proposed to be offered for trading on OTC Exchange have already been subscribed to by members and licensed dealers of OTCEI. CCI consent should also be obtained by the company to make the issue besides agreeing to abide by all statutory and OTCEI provisions for listing. The company must agree to enter into an agreement with the OTCEI in a prescribed format. It will be required to pay an initial listing fee of Rs. 6000/- and an annual fee of 0.01% of its subscribed capital for obtaining and continuing listing on the OTC Exchange of India.

OTCEI — A Critique

When the OTC concept first began crystallising into a concrete proposal in terms of OTCEI, the general feeling in the market was of positive expectation especially because it would open new vistas for profit and employment. However, despite the several anticipated advantages from the operations of the Exchange certain grey areas still remain.

The OTC Exchange is a remedy for the illiquidity of the scrips of smaller companies which are not sure of a good response to their public offers of equity. The scrips of these companies become more acceptable to the public with the backing of a member of the OTCEI acting as a sponsor. However, the responsibility of the sponsor is significant, especially because it has to certify that the scrip is investment worthy implying in a way that the company, its management and its product are al viable. One has yet to determine what the experience of the sponsor will be once the Exchange becomes operational and what the cost/benefit ratio of assuming such responsibility will be to the sponsor. This is a material point because the facility of over-the-counter trading is only a subsequent step.

Another point made by a financial expert in this regard merits consideration. All members of the proposed exchange and licensed dealers are to operate counters but this will come only after the completion of the project. The companies tapping the primary capital market do so to meet their investment requirements. They have to come up with a public offer of scrips well before the project gets completed.

if the OTC's involvement is only after project completion the promoter will have to seek financial resources on his own. While admitting that the investor's interests are better safeguarded by the OTC provision, it needs two parties to conduct business over the counter. Moreover, after a project is completed, the concerned company may not even need primary capital and may not want to sell scrips, though the investor may be interested. The sponsor is required to ensure full flow of investment funds which implies that several projects will be left high and dry.

Yet another clarification was sought in the financial circles. Companies listed on the OTCEI will be those falling within the capital ceiling of Rs. 3 crores and the minimum public offer of 10 per cent of the paid-up capital of Rs. 30 lacs whichever is less. There is no indication of the proportion of equity to be held by the management and the sponsoring institutions and whether there will be any provision for jobbers. Normally, it would be difficult to run a secondary market on a mere 10 per cent as there would be practically no floating stock available.

Finally, the issue of OTC market becoming a state monopoly has been raised. Although the OTC idea has been borrowed from its American counterpart, the NASDAQ, the concept and content of the idea have undergone some changes. The current proposal is that the OTC market will be established by financial institutions together with SBI Capital Markets and Canbank Financial Services. It is feared that this is bound to create a state monopoly in the capital markets. The government's preference for FIs may be in the belief that they will be fair and relatively scrupulous in making the deals which are struck in this market. By choosing only FIs for the operation of the OTC market, the government has ignored the irregularities (allegedly) perpetrated by the institutions in capital issues of companies in the recent past. Besides, even as the FIs and constituent bank funds of the OTC market will be playing the role of market-makers in scrips for companies and investors, they will be doing so by mopping up investible funds of the public. Promotion of mutual funds and schemes for investment have been the sole prerogative of nationalised banks in addition to the UTI and Insurance companies which together seem to have established a virtual hold on the secondary market. The question whether this virtual state control of the OTC market is desirable or not is debatable. The preference of the industrialists/entrepreneurs to list the shares of their companies in major stock exchange is yet to be pierced.

Conclusion

Originally, the OTCEI was to become operational from October, 1990 onwards. While several issues have since been sorted out such as members' list, capital structure, management and registered/corporate offices, the government clearance was expected in May 1991. OTCEI- which a different kind of stock exchange has launched as a company in 1992 under section 25 of the Indian Companies Act 1956 with the object of providing an opportunity to small companies to acquire public fund at low cost.

11

Deposit Insurance & Credit Guarantee Corporation – Performance & Prospects

T. N. K. Iyer

Introduction

The Deposit Insurance & Credit Guarantee Corporation has been collecting sizeable amount of premia, the rates of which was enhanced since 1.4.1989 from 0.5% to 1.5% per cent of total priority sector credit. This has naturally placed additional burden on banks since they have to absorb a proportion of the premia. Some private sector banks are reported to have even sought permission to withdraw from DICGCs guarantee scheme. Some of the State Financial Corporations have also reportedly been seeking to opt out on the ground that the DICGC has not been settling claims expeditiously. The DICGC, on its part, has been faced with the incidence of mounting claim burden, causing considerable strain on its resources. An attempt is made in this article to analyse the evolution and working of the DICGC.

The series of bank failures in the fifties and early sixties undermined the confidence of the depositors in the banking system. To restore the confidence of the public, the Government of India by an Act of parliament established the Deposit Insurance Corporation on

1.1.1962. Insurance of Bank deposit is intended to give a measure of protection to the depositors, particularly the smaller depositors from the risk of loss of their savings arising from Bank failures. The protection afforded by the Corporation by infusing confidence in the minds of the public contributes to the growth of the banking system by assessing in development of banking habits and mobilisation of resources by the banks which in turn can be utilised for purposes, as per national priority.

Similarly, in the wake of the social control measures initiated by the Government in 1968 followed by nationalisation of major commercial banks in July, 1969, the banks were required to ensure an increased flow of credit to small borrowers who find it difficult to have access to institutional credit. Though social control and other measures had created an awareness among banks of the need to provide more credit to the hitherto neglected category of borrowers, there was some hesitation among them to venture into new and riskier field of lending as also their inhibition to lend except against easily available security. With the experience gained by Reserve Bank of India from the operation of the Credit Guarantee Scheme for Small Scale Industries since 1960, the Credit Guarantee Corporation of India Ltd. was established as a public limited company on 14.1.1971 as an agency to provide a signal but wide ranging system of guarantees for loans granted by commercial banks and other financial institutions to small and needy borrowers.

The Merger of Two Corporations

The Deposit Insurance & Credit Guarantee Corporation of India as the organisation is known today is the result of the merger of these two independent organisation, namely the Deposit Insurance Corporation and the Credit Guarantee Corporation of India Ltd. The Deposit Insurance Corporation took over the undertaking of the Credit Guarantee Corporation of India with effect from July 1978 and was renamed as the Deposit Insurance & Credit Guarantee Corporation.

The objectives of corporation are twofold :

1. To provide for the benefit of persons having deposits in Banks, insurance against the loss of all or part of their deposits in all branches of a bank to maximum of Rs. 30,000/-, and
2. To provide guarantee support to credit extended to small borrowers by participating banks and other financial institutions and commercial banks, RRBs, Co-operative Banks, State Financial Corporations and other term lending institutions.

The credit guarantee scheme for small scale industries sponsored and formulated by the Government of India and administered by the Credit guarantee Organisation (Reserve Bank of India) since July 1960 was terminated by the Government in March 1981 and the DICGC introduced in its place a new scheme with effect from 1.4.1981 covering advances to small scale industries by commercial banks and other institutions. With the integration of the credit guarantee functions relating to small scale industries, the Corporation has been giving guarantee support to substantial amount of credit extended to the priority sectors. Pursuant to the recommendations of an Expert Committee appointed in 1987, the scope of the Credit Guarantee Schemes has been enlarged from 1.4.1989 to cover the entire gamut of priority sector advances as defined by Reserve Bank of India.

A Word About the New Definition of Priority Sector

With effect from 1.4.1989 the Small Loans Guarantee Scheme 1971 and Small Loans (Small Scale Industries) Guarantee Scheme 1981 will be applicable to the activities covered by the definition of priority sector as given by Reserve Bank of India (vide RBI circular RPCD NO. BC 29/PS 22-84 dated 16.3.1984). Accordingly, the credit facilities granted to (1) agriculture (2) small road and water transport operators (3) retail trade (4) small business (5) professional and self-employed persons (6) state sponsored organisation for SC/ST (7) education (8) housing and (9) consumption will be extended guarantee cover. Further indirect finance to agriculture, housing etc. will now be eligible for the guarantee cover.

Under Small Loans (Small Scale Industries) Guarantee Scheme, guarantee cover is now provided to (1) direct finance to small scale industries (2) indirect finance to small scale industries (3) and finance given for industrial estates. The indirect finance will include credit to (a) agencies involved in assisting the decentralised sector in the supply of inputs and marketing of output of artisans, village and cottage industries and (b) governments sponsored corporation/ organisations providing funds to the weaker sections in the priority sector.

The Salient Features of the Credit Guarantee Scheme

The Corporation is operating various credit guarantee schemes as detailed below :

1. Small Loans Guarantee Scheme, 1971
2. Small Loans (Financial Corporation) Guarantee Scheme, 1971
3. Service Co-operatives Societies Guarantee Scheme, 1971
4. Small Loans (Small Scale Industries) Guarantee Schemes, 1981
5. Small Loans (Co-operative Banks) Guarantee Scheme, 1984

1. The Small Loans Guarantee Scheme, 1971 came into forces with effect from 1.4.1971. It covers credit facilities granted by commercial banks including Regional Rural Banks to the priority sector as defined by Reserve Bank and this includes farmers and agriculturists, transport operators, retail traders, small business enterprises and professionals and self-employed persons.

2. The Small Loans (Financial Corporation) Guarantee Scheme, 1971 came into force on 1.7.1971 and covers credit facilities granted by State Financial Corporations to transport operators, hoteliers and other business enterprises engaged in generation or distribution of electricity, management/development of industrial estate etc.

3. The Service Co-operative Societies Guarantee Scheme came into force from 1.10.1971 and it covers among others credit facilities by all scheduled commercial banks and State and Central Co-operative Banks etc. to Service Co-operative Banks etc.

4. The Small Loans (Small Scale Industries) Guarantee Scheme 1981 introduced from 1.4.1981 covers credit facilities granted by commercial banks, RRBs, Co-operative Banks, State Financial Corporations etc. to small scale industrial units for acquisition of or repairs to or replacement of fixed assets requirements and for working capital requirements for production/sales etc.

5. The Small Loans (Co-operative Banks) Guarantee Scheme, 1984 which came into force from 1.7.1984 guarantee support to non-agricultural advances granted by primary (urban) co-operative banks to small borrowers etc.

Separate Funds

The Corporation which has an authorised capital of Rs. 50 crores subscribed entirely by Reserve Bank of India maintains separate funds for Deposit Insurance and for Credit Guarantees which are financed by the premia and guarantee fees received respectively and are utilised for meeting respective claims.

Premia for Deposit Insurance

Under the Deposit Insurance Scheme the insurance premium continued to be 4 paise per Rs. 100/- per annum.

Guarantee Fee for Priority Sector Advances

The guarantee fee for Small Loans Guarantee Scheme and Small Loans (SSI) Guarantee Scheme with effect from 1.4.1989 is payable on the banks total priority sector advances outstanding (excluding certain exempted category) as at the end of March every year as reported in the annual report of the bank. Guarantee fee is calculated at the rate of 1.5 per cent per annum and is payable annually before 30th April of the year either on adhoc or actual basis. In this connection, a view has been expressed that the published figures in Annual Report may include advances on which claims has already been received/lodged and the bank will still have to pay the guarantee fee, where as per the earlier instructions such advances were to be excluded for the purposes of calculating guarantee fee. Hence there may be possibility of excess payment of guarantee fee by banks. Further, with the change in the definition of priority sector by Reserve Bank of India an anomaly had crept in the coverage provide by DICGC. The anomaly could be stated as '*whatsoever are covered by Guarantee Schemes may not be priority sector advances and all the priority sector advances may not be covered by DICGC schemes*'. This has caused problems for banks for identifying priority sector advances for reporting to RBI and DICGC respectively.

Key Characteristics of Credit Guarantee Cover

The credit guarantee cover is available to those credit institutions which joins the schemes by entering into necessary agreements with the Corporation and paying the fee at prescribed rates. All eligible advances get automatically covered right from the date of the first disbursal without requiring the credit institution to make a fresh application to the Corporation for covering each credit facility. It is not therefore open to participating credit institutions to exclude any eligible credit facility from the purview of guarantee cover. To ensure that benefits of the guarantee scheme go to advance granted to small borrowers, several stipulations have been made in the guarantee scheme like ceiling on value of plant and machinery in case of small-scale units, ceiling on amount of credit as in case of retail traders, ceiling on value of equipment as in small business etc.

Extent of Guarantee Cover Under ...
a) Credit Guarantee Scheme

The amount of guarantee cover — varies as per different category of priority sector borrowers. In the case of small scale industries the maximum eligible amount is 60 per cent of the amount in default or Rs. 20 lakhs whichever is lower (Rs. 10 lakhs for term loan and Rs. 10 lakh for working capital), transport operators 60 per cent of amount in default or Rs. 1,50,000 whichever is lower, business enterprise —60 per cent of amount in default or Rs. 50,000/- whichever is lower, retail traders — 60 per cent of amount in default of Rs. 25,000/- whichever is lower, professional & self-employed persons — 60 per cent of amount in default or Rs. 50,000/- whichever is lower. In the case of agriculture advances also the eligible amount is 60 per cent of amount in default subject to overall ceiling of Rs. 60,000/- for more than one activity.

(b) Deposit Insurance : Extent of Insurance Cover

The extent of insurance cover under deposit insurance scheme in the event of liquidation, reconstruction or amalgamation of an insured bank is that every depositor of the insured banks is entitled to repayment of his deposits held by him in the same right and capacity of the bank upto a monetary ceiling of Rs. 30,000/-.

Invocation of Credit Guarantee

A credit institution has to comply with the following five conditions before a claim under the guarantee scheme can be preferred. These are:

(1) a minimum period of 3 years should lapse after grant of an eligible advance (newly stipulated)

(2) the guarantee fee due should have been paid on the entire priority sector advances outstanding as and when they became due,

(3) the advance under guarantee has not been repaid within one month from the date on which a note of demand for the repayment of entire dues has been served on the borrower,

(4) the advance is treated by the credit institution as bad or doubtful of recovery and, (5) it is provided or accounted for as such in the books of the credit institution.

Working of the Deposit Insurance Scheme

The deposit insurance scheme which came into operation in 1962 showed substantial progress over the years. The number of banks covered under the scheme increased from 276 in 1962 to 1921 in 1989-90.

In the following table the progress made under the deposit insurance scheme is presented.

Table 1

	1962	*1982*	*1987*	*1988-89*	*1989-90*
1. No. of insured banks	276	1683	1898	1903	1921
2. Assessable deposits (Rs. crores)	1895	42360	103044	126864	140746
3. Insured deposits (Rs. crores)	448	31774 (75.0)	75511 (73.3)	90192 (71.1)	101682 (72.2)
4. No. of accounts (in lacs)	77	1598	2598	2781	3142
5. No. of fully protected accounts (in lacs)	60	1581 (98.9)	2518 (98.0)	2705 (97.3)	3059 (97.4)
6. Claims paid (Rs. crores)	–	3	44	69	100

Note : (1) Figures in bracket under serial no. 3 indicated percentage of insured deposits to assessable deposits.

(2) Figures in bracket under serial no. 5 indicate percentage of fully protected accounts to total accounts.

It will be seen from the above table that though the assessable deposits and insured deposits have increased by 3 to 3.5 time between 1982 and 1989-90, insured deposits as percentage of assessable deposits have declined from 75 per cent in 1982 to 72.2 per cent in 19890-90. Similarly the percentage of fully protected accounts out of total number of accounts declined from 98.9 per cent to 97.4 per cent during the same period.

The insurance premium received by the Corporation during 1989-90 (1.4.89 to 31.3.90) amounted to Rs. 66.54 crores. However, as on 31.3.90, the total amount of claims paid so far in respect of 19 commercial banks (Rs. 97.55 crores) and 18 co-operative banks (Rs. 2.74 crores) totaled to Rs. 100.29 crores as against the figure of Rs. 69 crores as on 31.3.89. This spurt in payment was on account of the fact that the Corporation has to settle claims amounting to Rs. 31.42 crores in respect of Hindustan Commercial Bank Ltd., Delhi (amalgamated with Punjab National Bank) and United Commercial Bank Ltd., Calcutta (amalgamated with Allahabad Bank). In addition, 4 more commercial banks were placed under moratorium in August 1989. The actual liability of the Corporation in respect of these 4 banks is not known.

It will be seen that though claim paid by the Corporation was small upto 1982,. the cumulative amount of claim paid has increased substantially from Rs. 3 crores in 1984 to Rs. 100 crores in 1989-90, with prospects of more claims to be paid. Hence, it is likely the surplus the Corporation has been able to build-up over the years may decline gradually, if the present trends are of any indication.

Progress of Credit Guarantee Scheme

The number of credit institutions participating in the Corporations various credit guarantee schemes for small borrowers progressively increased over the years. Category-wise financial institutions participating in different guarantee schemes of the Corporation as on 31.3.89 and 31.3.90 are presented below.

Table 2

Category-wise Institutions Participating under Different Scheme

	Types of financial institutions							
	Commercial Bank		*RRBs*		*Co-operative Banks*		*Total*	
	31/3/89	31/3/90	31/3/89	31/3/90	31/3/89	31/3/90	31/3/89	31/3/90
1 Small Loans Guarantee Scheme 1971	71	67	196	196	196	–	267	263
2 Small Loans Financial Corporations Guarantee Scheme 1971	–	–	–	–	–	–	20	20
3 Service Cooperative Societies Guarantee Scheme	56	53	84	84	38	38	178	175
4 Small Lons (Cooperative Credit Societies Guarantee Scheme) 1982	–	–	–	–	–	-	–	–
5 Small Loans (Cooperative Banks) Guarantee Scheme 1984	–	–	–	–	86	89	86	89
Total							551	547

The number of commercial banks participating in the scheme declined from 267 to 263 on account of the amalgamation of the following 4 banks with four major nationalised banks, i.e. United Industrial Bank Ltd., Bank of Tamilnadu Ltd., Bank of Tanjavur Ltd., and Parur Central Bank Ltd.

The progress made under the credit guarantee scheme for small borrowers and small scale industries is presented in the following table :

Table 3

Progress of Credit Guarantee Scheme

(Amount Rs. crores)

	1972	*1982*	*1987*	*1988-89*	*1989-90*
1. Credit Guarantee Fund –	–	89	–	–	–
2. *Guaranteed Advances*					
(a) Small borrowers	208	4840	11116	14291	25586
(b) Small scales industries	–	3822	7738	10465	14094
Total	208	8662	18854	24756	39680
3. *Claim received for the year*					
(a) Small borrowers	–	25	255	364	356
(b) Small scales industries	–	30	149	241	199
Total	–	55	404	605	555
4. *Claim disposed for the year*					
(a) Small borrowers	–	15	225	281	347
(b) Small scales industries	–	27	122	177	388
Total	–	42	347	458	735

Guaranteed Advances

The total guaranteed advances under small borrowers scheme which were only Rs. 4840 crores in 1982 increased to Rs. 25586 crores in 1989-90 five fold increase in 7 years, while the total guaranteed advances under small loans (small scale industries) scheme increased from Rs. 3822 crores in 1982 to over Rs. 14094 crores in 1989-90 —

an increase of 3.7 times. Further, the increase in guaranteed advances under small borrowers scheme showed a sharp spurt between 1988-89 and 1989-90. The guaranteed advances under small loan scheme increased from Rs. 14291 crores in 1989-99 and 1989-90, showing an increase of 70 per cent over the previous year. The guaranteed advances to small scale industries also showed significant increase from Rs. 10465 crores to Rs. 14094 crores during the same period showing an increase of 34.7 pr cent compared to the previous year. This spurt in guaranteed advances was due to adoption of the 'Priority Sector' definition of Reserve Bank of India for the purpose of extending guarantee cover under various schemes from 1.4.1989.

Claims Received

The number of claims received by the Corporation during the year 1988-89 (15 months) were 1632, 927 for an aggregated amount of Rs. 605.17 crores while the number of claims received during the 12 months period ended 31.3.90 were 1579,257 for total claim amount of Rs. 554.37 crores (i.e. Rs. 555 crores).

Claims Settled

The Corporation settled 1704,712 credit guarantee claims for a total amount of Rs. 734.95 crores (say Rs. 735 crores) during the 12 months year ended 31.3.90, as compared to 1380,482 claims for Rs. 457.87 crores (say Rs. 458 crores) during the 15 months period ended 31.3.89. It will be evident from this that the claims disposed rate of the Corporation increased by about 55 per cent in number and 104 per cent in amount during the 12 months period ended 31.3.90 as compared to the 15 months period ended 31.3.89. This indicates that there is little substance in the arguments put forward by financial institutions that there is much delay in disposing applications by DICGC and they were not benefited.

Guarantee Fees Received

The mount of guarantee fees received by the Corporation during the period 1982 to 1989-90 under the Corporations various schemes are as follows.

Table 4
Guarantee Fee Received by the Corporation

(Rs. in crores)

	1982	*1987*	*1988-89 (15 months)*	*1989-90*
1. Small Loans Guarantee Scheme 1971	30.50	79.56	101.56	389.32
2. Small Loan (Financial Corporation) Guaranteed Scheme 1971	0.08	0.39	0.33	0.12
3. Service Co-operative Guarantee Scheme 1971	–	–	–	0.01
4. Small Loans (Co-operative Banks) GuaranteeScheme 1984	–	0.14	0.26	0.31
5. Small Loans (Small Scale Industries) Guaranteed Scheme	27.09	65.08	89.79	204.07
Total	57.67	145.17	191.89	593.83

The table above indicates there was a quantum jump in the guarantee fee receipt during the year ended 1989-90. Guarantee receipts increased from Rs. 145.17 crores in 1987 to over Rs. 593.83 crores in 1989-90 - an increase of over 4 times. This was partly due to increase in guarantee fee and partly due to the large increase in guaranteed advances as per the extended definition of priority sector adopted from 1.4.1989.

Category-wise, guarantee receipt under Small Loans Guarantee Scheme increased from Rs. 79.56 crores in 1987 to Rs. 389.32 crores - an increase by 4.9 times while guarantee fee under Small Loans (Small Scale Industries) Guarantee Scheme increased from Rs. 65.08 crores to Rs. 204.70 crores - an increase by 3.1 times during the same period.

It is common knowledge that the Credit Guarantee Scheme was running at a loss in view of the ever increasing claims lodged by financial institutions. The corporation had to shift the surplus from the Deposit Insurance Fund to the Guarantee Fund to pay for the guarantee claims. The credit guarantee fund disclosed net deficit of Rs. 264.72 crores as on 3.12.1987 and Rs. 148.99 crores as on 31.3.89, which had been adjusted against the surplus of Rs. 348.85 crores and Rs. 220.85 crores respectively available in the deposit insurance fund as on these dates. Subsequent to the enhancement of the guarantee fee, the credit guarantee fund as on 31.3.90 disclosed a net surplus of Rs. 188.64 crores and the same was transferred to Deposit Insurance fund. Even after this transfer a sum of Rs. 225.07 crores is due to the deposit insurance fund.

A cursory look at the figure presented in the table-5 will indicate that it is the financial institutions which have benefited more from DICGC.

It will be seen from the table-5 that the DICGC was incurring heavy losses during 1987 and 1988-89. The published profits of the banking sector for the year ended March 1990 was Rs. 302.40 crores, while the claim amount settled by DICGC were Rs. 735 crores (Small Loans Rs. 347 crores plus SSI borrowers Rs. 388 crores). The actual claim amount paid during the year was Rs. 515.44 crores composed of Rs. 338.52 crores under Small Loans plus Rs. 176.92 crores under Small Scale Industries. This shows it is DICGC which was subsidising the banks to show profits and the banks have only benefited by the DICGC. Though the guarantee fee receipts have shown a surplus during the year ended 31.3.90 it is not sure whether the total amount of guarantee receipts obtained during 1989-90 will be maintained for the year ended 31.3.91, in view of the exemption of certain category of advances like export advances granted to small scale industries for the purpose of payment of guarantee fee for the year 1990-91. Also no guarantee fee is to be paid on non-fund based limits like letters of credit, co-acceptances, financial guarantees and bills discounted under IDBI bill rediscounting scheme.

Table 5

Guarantee Fee Received and Total Claim Paid

Year	*Guarantee fee receipt*	*Claims paid under small borrowers*	*Claims paid under SSI including Govt. Scheme*	*Total claims paid*
1982	57.67	12.49	14.99	27.48
1985	105.66	71.80	24.98	96.78
1987	145.17	141.92	95.41	237.33
1988-89 (15 months)	191.89	272.29	104.71	376.46
1989-90	593.83	338.52	176.92	515.44

A recent study made by DICGC regarding institution group-wise analysis of the operations of all the credit guarantee schemes of DICGC for the period 1986 to 1988-89 (March 1989) reveal very interesting information. The share of various institutions in guarantee fee, claims lodged, paid and pending are given below.

Table 6

Institution Group-wise Guarantee Fee Received and Claims Paid

(Rs. in crores)

	Guarantee fee	Claims lodged	Claims paid	Ratio of guarantee fee to claims paid	Claims pending
SBI group	153.71	426.20	240.03	1:1.56	101.26
Nationalised Banks	280.23	617.43	391.00	1:1.40	162.51
Private Banks	17.93	38.15	18.37	1:1.02	11.25
Foreign Banks	1.21	0.25	0.19	1:0.16	0.12
RRBs	28.73	97.92	81.52	1:2.84	34.79
State Financial Corporations	13.86	60.26	27.63	1:1.99	40.51
Co-operative Banks	5.99	7.05	1.66	1:0.28	4.82
Total	501.66	1247.26	760.40	1:1.52	355.26

The above data clearly bring into prominence the fact that Regional Rural Banks, State Financial Corporations, SBI Groups, Nationalised Banks, Private Sector Banks come in the order of the maximum beneficiaries under the scheme. Foreign Bank and Co-operative Banks were the least beneficiaries. Thus as against total guarantee fee of Rs. 501.66 crores collected during the period 1986 to 1988-89, the Corporation has paid Rs. 760.40 crores by way of claims to various financial institutions. This study nullifies the arguments put forward by banks that they are the loosers under the credit guarantee scheme.

It is not known widely that the guarantee claims received by DICGC has more than doubled between 1987 and 1989-90. They have crossed the one and half million mark in 1989-90 as will be evident from the table-below.

Table 7

Claims Received by DICGC

(Rs. in crores)

	1982		*1987*		*1988-89*		*1989-90*	
	Nos.	*Amt.*	*Nos.*	*Amt.*	*Nos.*	*Amt.*	*Nos.*	*Amt.*
Under Small Loans Small Borrowers	150926	24.71	630365	140.94	1071221	255.27	1528391	364.07
Under Small Loans Small Scale Industries (1981)	4013	9.40	44711	131.68	93716	216.90	74894	192.58
Under Governemet SSI Scheme (now cancelled)	10447	20.53	4870	17.39	10820	24.20	1014	6.04

As on 31.3.1990 the grand total number of claims received under Credit Guarantee Scheme relating to Small Borrowers since inception of the scheme were 6012,464 for total amount of Rs. 1403.12 crores. Similarly as on 31.3.90 the grand total of claims received under Credit guarantee Scheme for Small Industries (including Government Schemes) since inception were 399,898 numbers for total amount of Rs. 1068.22 crores.

The data presented above reveals the ever increasing trends in claim receipts under small borrowers and small scale industries scheme. As for example, claim receipts increased from 630,356 (nos.) in 1987 to 1528,391 (nos.) in 1988-89 under small borrowers scheme. In case of small scale industries the number of claims under both schemes (Corporation and Government) increased from 49,581 in 1987 to over 75,900 in 1989-90.

This phenomenal increase in lodgment of claim receipts with DICGC reflects a deterioration in the quality of loan portfolios of financial institutions. The recovery performance of public sector banks in respect of their direct agricultural lending is far from satisfactory. In respect of small scale industries the increasing incidence of industrial sickness has been reflected in the large increase in the number of credit guarantee claims lodged with DICGC.

Out of 23.75 lakh SSI borrowal units availing of bank credit amounting to Rs. 11,415 crores as at end of June 1988, 2.17 lakh accounts with outstanding bank credit of Rs. 1980 crores have been identified by banks as sick. Out of this only 8,347 units with outstanding of Rs. 336.25 crores were reported to be under nursing programme. The number of non-viable units were 1.99 lacs with outstanding bank credit of Rs. 1,398 cores. In these cases the banks will have no alternative but to lodge claims at one time or another with DICGC. The reasons for the sharp increase in the number of claims lodged are many.

1. Instead of production/income oriented advances, more emphasis was on attaining targets in respect of mass loans, advances under DRI, SEPUP, SEEUY, IRDP schemes - a large percentage of borrowers under these schemes were found to be defaulters and the recovery was meager. This was partly unavoidable on account of Government directives.

2. Lack of proper appraisal of small borrowers/small scale industries projects by financial institutions either due to ignorance/lack of expertise/or the desire to achieve targets by taking over weak accounts from other banks.

3. Untimely and inadequate finance provided to small scale industries-more specially when they show signs of incipient sickness.

4. Lack of proper monitoring resulting in failure to detect incipient sickness in SSI accounts etc. and delay in taking decision for revival/nursing.

5. Repercussion on recovery of other advances subsequent to waiver of small agricultural loan etc. upto Rs. 10,000/-.

The cumulative effect of the above facts are reflected in the ever increasing number of sticky/sick small borrower/small scale industries accounts resulting in non-recovery of dues and lodgment of claims with DICGC. It is, therefore, but natural that confronted with very large number of claims, DICGC is not able to expeditiously settle claims as decided by financial institution. For instance in respect of small scale industries claim amounting to Rs. 29.57 crores are pending over 1 year out of total claim of Rs. 90.79 crores as on 31.3.90. This constitute 32 per cent of the total claims pending and cannot be considered large, considering the phenomenal increase in claim lodgment. In order to stem the large increase in claim receipt, DICGC has now stipulated minimum 3 year locking period before lodging claim.

The solution to this problem is not withdrawal of membership by financial institutions from DICGC as suggested by some bankers. Creation of separate insurance fund by respective financial institutions as a substitute for credit guarantee under DICGC has its own demerits. If every financial institutions creates its own insurance fund, appropriation of the insurance fund to settle the claim of sick accounts of the bank may create problems like personal intervention of interested persons in the institution. A third party administering the fund as is done by DICGC at present appears to be better arrangement than a creation individual funds by banks.

There is however an important factor to be considered. The guarantee cover extended by DICGC over the years has created a sense of complacency among bank managers and staff while appraising and monitoring of borrowal accounts. To some extent the increase failures of small borrowal/small scale industries accounts appears to be on account of improper appraisal of loan applications and lack of effective monitoring after disbursal of the loan. Management of financial institution should streamline their credit administration system, in order to stem the ever rowing failures of small borrowal accounts. Only when he credit appraisal system improves at branch/Regional/Zonal/ Head Office level and effective monitoring of loan accounts implemented, will it be possible for the financial institutions to improve their credit portfolio and reduce their non-performing assets. This in turn will lessen the claim on DICGC, and enable it to reduce the guarantee fee. On its part, DICGC can on the basis of experience gained, give appropriate guidelines to financial institutions to administer their credit portfolio effectively and also effect change in its rules and regulations in keeping with the emerging situation.

Another suggestion which merit consideration is that the banks and other financial institutions may delink advances to small borrowers and small scale industries from the credit guarantee scheme, five years after the initial disbursal provided they are not sticky or sick. After all small enterprises/small industries require more support during the initial teething period only as the mortality is highest during the initial 4/5 years. After ceasing to pay the guarantee fee on such delinked accounts, the financial institution may recover at least 1 per cent by way of additional interest (instead of 1.5 per cent Guarantee fee) and create a separate reserve fund. This will enable the banks to make provision for sick/non-performing accounts after they are delinked from credit guarantee scheme. This scheme can satisfy both the financial institutions and DICGC.

12

Credit Risk Management in Banks

K. Ram Mohan

Introductory

The process of liberalisation and deregulation in the banking sector began with the initiation of financial sector reforms and rightly the 90s have come to be a decade of the "second revolution" in Indian banking. There has been a marked shift in ideology as evident from the emphasis in favour of prudential regulation instead of structural regulation. The barriers to entry into the financial sector have been relaxed with the objective of fostering healthy competition among the participants. This in turn, is expected to correct the distortions built into the system through the interventionist policies earlier and the resultant inefficiencies in allocation of resources. In order to achieve this objective, progressive deregulation of interest rate has been carried out and the risk-reward perception is slowly being inculcated among the banks. At the same time, with the implementation of income recognition and provisioning norms, banks have started evaluating the credit weaknesses in loan assets and indirectly they are taking the role of risk-assessors. With competition gaining momentum, the market is likely to get highly segmented resulting in squeeze in profit margins. In order to protect their market share and their profit, banks can be expected to undertake high risk-high return activities which they may not have earlier. Therefore, it can be logically concluded that the risk perception will come to play a major role in credit decisions made by banks.

Move Towards Asset-Liability Management

The movement towards risk-reward process of allocation of financial resources has already begun. As part of deregulation of interest rates, the system of Prime Lending Rate (PLR) has already been introduced under which banks are expected to be 'price makers' and quote the interest rates for loans depending upon their risk perception. Theoretically, in a competitive milieu, to be a successful price maker, the banks will have to critically analyse the inherent credit risks attached to each credit decision. Whether the Indian banks have the wherewithal at present to undertake such task is a critical question. Bank have already implemented their prime lending rates, although the methodology of arriving at the PLR is also a matter of debate. It would appear to be driven by consideration of where 'market leaders' like SBI and few of the large public sector banks fix their PLR.

Secondly, as part of the Memorandum of Understanding (MOU), public sector banks are required to evolve a "Loan Policy" where banks are required to evolve proper pricing policies for loans.

Thirdly, the system of bifurcation of working capital into cash credit and loan component (following the recommendations of the Jilani Committee) in case of borrowers with a credit limit of Rs. 20 crore and above has been introduced. Eventually this concept can be expanded and it can be expected that the system of roll-over credit will be replaced with loans of fixed maturity. With further deregulation of interest rates, this will facilitate matching of assets with liabilities, depending upon their maturity profiles. Banks can be expected to further this process to eventually evolve Asset-Liability Management (ALM) function aimed at managing the risks appropriately and maximising the spread available.

Leaving aside the question whether complete deregulation of interest rates is possible in the Indian context, one can state with reasonable certainty that barring a few concessional rates of interest for the directed credit programmes, banks will be more or less free to decide their interest rate structure based on their cost of funds and return thereof. The present structural rigidity in the money market could also get rectified to facilitate the emergence of a 'anchor rate' upon which all other interest rate will come to be determined and which will result in banks adopting the system of floating and fixed interest rates on assets and liabilities. No doubt, this will call for financial sophistry; but it is within the realm of possibility in the Indian context.

Concept of Credit Risk

At the present juncture, the prudential accounting norms have heightened the risk awareness among banks only in a limited way. However, if we go by the scenario portrayed above, banks will have to address various risks if they have to remain profitable. Keeping this in view, a taxonomy of risks is described below.

According to the Committee on General Terminology of the American Risk and Insurance association, risk is defined as "uncertainty as to the outcome of an event when two or more possibilities exist". From a lender's point of view, this definition is equally valid as the two probabilities of success and failure of a venture may results in either repayment or default of a loan. Risk management in credit is vital since in the event of a loss, the lender will take quite a long time to recover the loss. For example, if the profit margin of a lender is 4%, to recoup a loan loss of Rs. 100, it will take 25 long years, if an equivalent money is successfully deployed in a performing loan! Basically, credit risk is the risk of default or delayed or fragmented repayments leading to an additional cost element to the lender and making the loan nonviable. Since the concept of credit risk boils down to a single question as to whether the loan is repaid as scheduled or not, some experts view 'default risk' synonymously with credit risk. However, it is felt that a more holistic view should be taken since, various kinds of risks interplay simultaneously and one form of risk may lead to another, ultimately resulting in default. Therefore, as a prudent banker, it is imperative that risk analysis of any credit decision should atleast look for some major forms of risk that influence repayments directly and considerably.

A Taxonomy of Risk

Although the list is not exhaustive, the following 'risks' play an important role in leading to credit risk.

(a) Liquidity risk is the first and foremost that a banker will be looking for, as it covers the ability of the borrower to meet the repayment commitments in time. Should the borrower turn ill-liquid, the banker may face the risk of ill-liquidity leading to bankruptcy. Hence, under this, both adequacy of cash flow and the likelihood of the customer turning bankrupt are analysed.

(b) Financial risk is what banks at present analyse predominantly. It encompasses the systematic analysis of various financial ratios, balance sheet of the borrower, trading and P&L account, funds-flow etc. so that meaningful conclusions can be drawn about the ability of the borrower to repay a loan.

(c) Cost-base risk indicates the degree of income or profit generated within a unit from a given cost structure. As business develops, the marginal cost usually decreases upto a level after which it rises again. It is important that the banker analyses the cost-base threshold from where costs rise, to ensure that the projections made by he borrower are relevant. Other factors like under-utilised capacity, level of inventory etc. are also considered for the purpose.

(d) Default risk is the main risk that bankers are concerned with and is divided into two components viz., probability to pay and propensity to repay. While the former refers to the adequacy of cash flow to make the repayment, the latter relates to the intention of the borrower to repay the loan.

(e) Fiduciary risk covers all credit risks attached to off-balance sheet items of the borrower. For instance, in case of a LC or LG lines of credit, the capability of the borrower to meet these commitments in time will be crucial as otherwise it will convert itself into a fund-based commitment for the banker.

Credit Risk Management

Basically, credit risk management encompasses a systematic analysis of various forms of risks that directly or indirectly influence or likely to influence the repayment of a loan given by the bank. Unlike in the conventional credit appraisal methods practiced at present, credit risk management calls for systematic probe into the nature of business, projections made by the borrower, management of men, machines and material as well as the business environment for identifying the extent of different risks. Thereafter, holistic view is taken by integrating the various risks perceived; the loan offer is thus rated as to whether the interplay of risks are well within the acceptable levels of the bank.

The approaches to credit risk management which are commonly used world over are both qualitative and quantitative. The qualitative approach include industry comparison and attribute analysis, while quantitative techniques cover probabilistic scenario building, simulation and statistical analysis. The fundamental difference between the present appraisal of credit proposals and credit risk analysis lies in the fact that the former is a static analysis whereas in the later, a dynamic approach is made by creating various probabilistic scenarios and analysing the interplay of various internal and external forces so as to derive a holistic view.

Under the qualitative approach, risk analysis is carried out comparing the financial ratios of the unit with that of the industry, in order to understand where exactly the borrower fits in the industry. For the purpose, usually, industry averages are done in five scale classification of Upper Quartile (Very Good), Quartile (Good), Median (Average (arrived as an average of upper quartile and median) and Lower quartile.

In attribute analysis, various interacting factors are structured as a questionnaire and some predetermined weights are used to convert the indices given by the analyst so that a qualitative opinion on the risk content of the proposal can be made. Depending on the quantum of exposure, risk analysis is made using any of the above or all techniques.

Under quantitative technique, credit risk is statistically measured as the Standard Deviation of the various probabilistic scenarios created. This represents the most probable extent of deviation, measured under various probabilistic scenarios including the most pessimistic situations created from a given projection. If the cash flow surplus is sufficient to meet repayment and also the standard deviation (representing credit risk), then in all probability, the borrower will be in a position to meet his commitments, even in an adverse situation.

Tools of Analysis

Qualitative and quantitative credit risk analysis make use of several investigative tools and some of the predominantly used tools are described below. The list, it may be noted is not exhaustive but only indicative. Depending on the complexity of the credit proposal and the ingenuity of the analyst, details of risk analysis can vary. What is important is that the analysis should lead to logical conclusions in evaluating the risk content in a credit decision.

As mentioned earlier, in quantitative techniques, statistical method of standard deviation is predominantly used to measure credit risk. Apart from this, there are various scoring models like the altman model, Richard Taffler model, Howard Tisshaw model, Deakin model etc. These are basically predictive models, and are based on Multiple Discriminant Analysis (MDA) functions and are generally held to have universal applicability. In the Indian condition also some of the models are seen to have a good predictive capability. MDA is an advanced statistical method used to analyse multivariate characteristics germane to a group membership and is used to categories an classify the results of multivariate observations in a group/class.

Other quantitative approaches include Classification and Regression Tree (Chart), Regression Partition Analysis (RPA) - Tree technique, LOGIT analysis, definite pay-back period method, addition of a risk premium to the Discounted Cash Flow, risk cushion analysis etc.

Qualitative tools on the other hand, use extensively various financial ratios, analysis of strength of primary and collateral securities, authenticity of financial statements, sensitivity analysis etc. These are being adopted by the banks in one form or other. Under attribute analysis mentioned earlier, compared to the practice of analysing the sales and profit growth, risks perceived from various parameters and their interaction during the course of normal businesses are analysed through a structured questionnaire. Since this is a subjective analysis, in order to minimise subjectivity, a wide scale of 10 for each close ended question is prescribed.

The discussion above provides a broad overview of the issues in credit risk management. Suggested working models for evaluating working capital risk (Work-risk) and project financing risk (Projrisk) that may be readily used in day-to-day operations is provided in annexure.

The development of such models is usually labour-intensive and long drawn. However, with the availability of computers the task has been made quite simple as standardised packages can be easily developed suiting the needs and the policies of the bank. However it needs to be added that such computer-based credit risk models are only decision support system and cannot replace the human judgement involved in any credit decision.

As banks shift from the earlier security-based financing through cash-credit system to cashflow based short term finance and lines of credit, there will be a crucial need for evolving risk management practices. Moreover, the ALM function bereft of such analysis would be less effective. With competition picking up, there will be need for three distinct functions viz., credit marketing, risk analysis and credit administration. For sake of efficiency, it would be useful to keep these functions independent with clear reporting relationships.

Annexure

Working Models for Credit Risk Analysis

Working Capital Risk Analysis ;

The working capital risk (WORK RISK) in a credit proposal can be analysed by comparing the important ratios of the proposal with that of the industry, evaluating the strength of the financial statements, primary and collateral securities of fered and the risk profile of the industry per se. After this, the risk on account of external forces are evaluated through the attribute analysis.

In case of big borrowal accounts, in addition to the above a more detailed quantitative analysis for various forms of risks can be attempted as under :

Nature of Risk	**suggested tools**
Bankruptcy Risk	MDA scoring models like Altman. Taffler, Ram Avtar, Howard Tisshaw etc.,
Liquidity Risk	CART-Analysis of Altman, Frydman and Kao.
Default Risk	Chesser's LOGIT model, RPA Tree analysis suggested by Srinivasan, Venkat & Kim.
Cost Base Risk	Substainability Growth analysis and Coleshaw's working worth model.

After analysing the various aspects of credit risk in a proposal, the predictions are then integrated, so that a holistic view can be taken. Such a detailed analysis will clearly bring out the weak spots in the proposal, which has to be adequately taken care of by proposing suitable covenants at the time of sanction.

Normally for working capital risk analysis, the last two years actuals, along with current year estimates and next year projections, as is provided in the existing CMA formats, should suffice. From this, for each type of risk, we can get four year-wise predictions and also the overall trend that is likely to emerge on the basis of past two years and the current year estimate. Since in case of working capital, annual review is being done, the predictions are limited to only the next year, unlike in the case of project credit risk analysis, which normally involves a longer period.

Tools Used in this Model

Having briefly seen the suggested model of risk analysis, let us look at the various suggested tools that are referred above.

Liquidity risk and the bankruptcy risk are measured using various Z-Score models that are of well proven. Instead of basing the risk evaluation on a single model, usually the credit analyst uses more than one model, so that his prediction can be broad-based. The oldest and celebrated Z-score model is that developed by Altman (1983) and the later version of the same is as under :

Z = 0.717 X1 + 0.847 X2 + 3.107 X3 + 0.420X4 + 0.998 X5., Where

X1 = Working capital/Total Assets. (Measure of liquidity)

X2 = Retained Earnings/Total Assets (Measure of reinvested earnings)

X3 = Earnings Before Interest and Tax/Total Assets (Profit-ability measure)

X4 = Book value of Equity/Book value of Total Debts. (Measure of leverage)

X5 = Sales/Total Assets (Measure of sales generating ability of Assets)

Z = Over-all Index.

The cut off points suggested is, if Z>3.00, good, and if it is below 2.09 it is risky. The Z score of>2.09, but <3.00 is called a grey zone, where additional analysis is necessary.

Under the Indian context, Mr. Ram Avatar Yadav (1986) has developed a scoring model to measure the liquidity and bankruptcy risks and has come out with a Y score model as under :

Y-Score = 19.8927 X1 + 0.0047 X2 + 0.07141 X3 + 0.4860 X4, Where,

X1 = Earnings before Interest and Tax/Total Tangible Assets (Measure of productivity of assets)

X2 = Current Asset/Current Liability (Measure of iliquidity of the company)

X3 = Net Sales/Total tangible Assets (Measure of assets turn-over)

X4 = ** Defensive Assets/Total Operating Expenses (Defensive interval ratio)

by operating expenses minus depreciation, depletion and amortisation (as they are not current drain on cash and its equivalent). This is a measure of interval of time for which the company can finance its continuing operations, without addition of asset or payment of liabilities.

A Y-Score of 1.52 and more is indicative of sound health of the company and Y-Score of less than 1.33 is indicative of high risk company. If it is between 1.33 and 1.52, this is called an area of ignorance or uncertainty, where further analysis is necessary.

Subseq ent to analysis of liquidity/bankruptcy risks, liquidity risk can be analysed. For this purpose, a model suggested by Chesser and Delton based on the probability of the repayment is not only default in repayment, but also any work-out (rescheduling) that might have been arranged resulting in a settlement of the loan less favourable to the lender than the original agreement. The statistical technique used here is called as LOGIT and is similar to MDA and considers the following six variables :

X1 = (Cash + Marketable securities)/Total assets.

X2 = Net Sales/(Cash + Marketable securities)

X3 = EBIT/Total Assets.

X4 = Total Debt/Total Assets.

X5 = Fixed Assets/Net Worth.

X6 = *Working capital/Net Sales.

From this a variable "Y", which is a linear combination of the independent variables, including intercept is derived as under :

Y = - 2.043 + (-5.21) X1 + 0.0053 X2 + (-6.6507) X3 + 4.4009 X4 + (-0.0791) X5 - 0.1020 X6.

According to Chesser, under his LOGIT model, the probability of non-compliance "P", can be computed using the formula :

$P = 1/1 + e^{-y}$

Where exponential "e" is 2.71828. If "P" >0.50 assign it to non - = compliance group, and if it is <0.50 assign it to compliance group. Thus the "Y" can be viewed as the borrower's probability of non-compliance.

Another important indicative tool (which may be suitably altered to suit to the individual needs of the bank) is the Working worth and Balance Sheet Rating Model suggested by Cloeshaw. According to him, working worth of a company can be computed as under :

$$\text{Working worth} = \frac{\text{Working capital + net worth}}{2}$$

This is a measure of 'size' of a company, not in terms of turnover, but in relation to the levels of working funds and its 'paper value' (i.e., the level of finance upto which credit risk is within bank's acceptable level)

The balance sheet rating is computed by him as under :

Balance sheet rating = X1+ X2 - X3 -= X4, where,

S1 = Current Asset/Current Liability.

X2 = (Current Asset-Stock)/ Current Liabilities.

X3 = Current Liabilities/ New Worth.

X4 = Total Liabilities /Net Worth.

Ratios X1 & X2 are the common current and quick liquidity measures, while ratios X3 & X4 are common gearing ratios. A decision matrix of balance-sheet strength versus working worth is used for arriving at a credit decision. According to him, the scales can be adjusted based on experience and corporate policies of the lender. Such a measure can also act as a benchmark for fixing limits and thereby paves way for a uniform judgement in credit appraisal.

Project Risk Analysis Model

In case of project risk (PROJRISK), in addition to the default and liquidity risks, additional care has to be taken as this covers usually a longer time period ranging from 5 years and up-wards. For this using the *sensitivity analysis or what if* analysis we can create a number of probabilistic scenarios, most of which being pessimistic, so that from the distribution of these projected scenarios, we can compute the Standard deviation of cash flows. From discounted cash flows, we have to compute the Net Asset Value for various time periods and if the same are positive even after adjustment for the standard deviation of the cash flow, then we can say that the borrower wili have enough to repay the bank's instalments. In other words, instead of arbitrarily assigning a value for the risk factor, under this technique, we try to logically quantify the same.

Bibliography

1. K. Ram Mohan Under Guidance of Prof. A. K. Sen Gupta, "Risk Analysis in Credit Appraisal and Credit Rating : Inland and Foreign Financing.", BMP XIV, dissertation submitted to MIBM, Pune, (1992-93).

2. Edward I Altman, "Corporate Bankruptcy Predictions and its Implications for commercial Loan Evaluation", *Journal of Commercial Bank Lending, Jan., 1970.*

3. Yadav, Ram Avtar, *Financial Ratios and the Predictions of corporate failure,* Concept Publishing Company, New Delhi, Published in 1986.

4. John Coleslaw, "Credit Analysis", Wood Head - Faulkner England, 1989.

13

Lease Financing

B. L. Mathur

In modern time, leasing has become an unique mode of financial use of assets. Leasing as financing concept is simple-an arrangement between two parties, the leasing company or the lessor and the úser or the lessee, whereby the former arranges to buy capital equipment for the use of the latter in accordance with the latter's requirement and specifications. There are two parties involved in leasing-the lessor, who owns and finances the purchase of the assets, and the lessee, to whom the assets is rented. The right of use of the assets is vested to lessee for a price, i.e., payment of rent at regular intervals. Under the lease agreement, lessee use the assets without any capital investment in it. Normally the rent of the assets is payable in advance at periodic intervals agreed by the lessor and lessee. Leasing having a fixed period and normally it is form three to five years. But in this regard much is depends upon the type of the equipment. The period of lease agreement may be classified in two categories- primary period and secondary period. The initial period of the lease agreement is known as the "primary period" whereas the period after renewal of agreement is known as "secondary period". During the primary period, the lessor normally ables to recover his entire investment and his profit. At the expirty of the primary period, it is customary that lessee gives an option to lessor for renewal of the lease agreement at a nominal rentals.

The main reason behind the charging of nominal rent by the lessor is that till the end of secondary period the lessor has recovered his investment as well as margin. In practice, it is found that at the end of the primary period the lessor prefer to sold the assets to the lessee. The lessee also arranges for payments of insurance and for maintenance of the assets.

Types of Lease

The lease transactions generally fall into one of the following four categories:

(i) Operating Lease
(ii) Financial Lease
(iii) Sale-and-Lease-back transactions
(iv) The leveraged Lease

Operating Leases: The concept of the operating lease is a familiar one. It refers to a short-term lease of an asset, generally, a computer or an air conditioner for hire for a limited time period, sometimes for even one day, or the hire of a car, for which the per hour or per day rental is very much higher than for the assets which are leased for a period of five/six years, for the risk of ownership and non-use of the assets rests with the Owner/Lessor.

Financial Lease: The International Accounting Standard committee has defined financial lease as "a lease that transfers substantially all the risks and rewards incident to ownership of an asset. Title may or may not eventually be transferred. In financial lease, the contract is irrevocable during the primary period and the rentals payable during that period will be adequate enough to recover the total investment of the lessor in the asset. In a financial lease, lessor chooses and purchase the assets on the instructions of the lessee and lessor finances for that assets. The lessor also pays the amount of assets on behalf of the lessee. While preparing the accounts, the lessor will show the assets in his account and also claim depreciation for that, it is also known as full pay lease.

The financial lease has the following characteristics:

* It provides for a basic term during which the lease is non-cancellable. The length of his basic lease period is determined primarily by the economic life of the asset, and is usually somewhat shorter than expected life.

* It provides for periodic rental payments during this period, which are calculated on the basis of the return of the original investment in the asset to the investor, and which provides him with a pre-determined rate of return.

* The cost of insurance, maintenance and other related expenses are debited to the account of the lessee.

* The lessee customarily provides some means by which the company may continue to use the assets, after the expiration of the basic lease period. Alternatively, following termination, a market purchase price is negotiable.

Sale-and Lease-Back Transactions: This transaction provides for an arrangement by which an entity that owns a given asset may sell it to the leasing company, and lease it back. This enables the lessee to immediately defreeze the money that he has locked into the original asset, which becomes available to him for working capital for further expansion.

Leveraged Lease: The lease arrangement is completed when very large assets are to be purchased, such as a nuclear power plant, desalination units, etc. No one lessor is comfortable in committing the entire purchase price of the assets, nor can one lessor absorb the depreciation benefits thrown out by the ownership of the asset. Accordingly, several parties come together to acquire the asset, and lease it to a lessee.

Advantages and Disadvantages

The leasing of an asset instead of its outright purchase has the following advantages from the Lessee's point of view:—

1. As there is no down payment except one instalment of rent which is usually paid in advance. It enables acquisition of fixed assets without any initial investment on the part of the lessee.

2. As the leased equipment and the corresponding rental obligations do not form part of the assets and liabilities of the lessee Company in their balance sheet, the Company borrowing capacity remain unaffected on account of leasing. This fact has, however, lost of its importance today, as modern accounting practices have recognized the need to indicate the details of leased equipment by way of notes to the balance sheets of lessees and financial analysts take into account the future rentals payable as part of the contingent liabilities of the lessee. Leasing, However, still remains an additional source of term finance to industry which leaves unimpaired their resource of borrowings.

3. As the entire lease rentals can be claimed as business expenditure by the lessee, for industries/concerns subject to high rates of taxation, leasing may turn out to be financially attractive. Under leasing, the cost of equipment is paid from pre-tax profits/own funds of the Company towards the initial margin and for repayment of loans subsequently.

4. Under leasing, the cost of an asset i.e. lease rentals can be paid out of the additional cash generated from the use of the same asset. It is, therefore, possible to match the timing of cash outflows and inflows on account of the acquisition of a particular asset.

5. As the Lease rentals are fixed for the entire duration of the contract, there is certainty about the lessees to plan their finances.

6. The acquisition of assets under leasing is much simpler compared to the delay and procedural work involved in raising term borrowing from institutions and banks or raising capital from the

market in India. Moreover, the various regulations and convents to be adhered to in case of term borrowings from the institutions or market issues of capital can be avoided by going in for leasing.

7. The cost of leased equipment is precisely quantified and therefore lessees will be more concerned about making full use of the equipment where the opportunity cost of lower capacity utilisation may not be so evident.

8. Leasing can take care of normal replacement/acquisition of balancing equipment, etc. by industries thereby enabling them to conserve their own funds for deploying in major expansion/diversification schemes or for strengthening their liquid position. In Europe and United State, however, leasing is undertaken even on a larger scale for financing acquisition of aircraft's, ships, oil drilling equipments, etc. But the major scope for leasing remains in the sphere of industrial plant and machinery and road transport equipment.

However, Leasing of equipment, instead of their outright purchase is not without following disadvantages:

1. Leasing is not suitable mode of project finance. This is because rentals are payable soon after entering into the lease contract while in new projects cash generations may start only after a fairly long gestation period.

2. Owning will be a better alternative than leasing for assets whose value is likely to appreciate over a period of time, such as land, buildings, etc. on the other hand, for equipment subject to fast rate of obsolescence, leasing will be a better alternative to purchasing.

3. Certain tax benefits/incentives such as backward area benefits may not be available on leased equipment.

4. Under financial lease, the lessee will not be in a position to terminate the contract except by paying heavy penalties. This may prove to be a handicap for manufacturers when they want to discontinue a particular line of business. In case of owned assets the manufacturers can sell the equipment at the time of winding up.

Development of the Concept

The leasing concept, as a financial facility had its origin in the United States of America, is gathering momentum in developed and developing countries. U. S. A. Rail and Roadways Corporation used the leasing for financing their rolling stocks. Thereafter, the concept in its present form became popular in U. K. In the United States, the first major leasing company known as US Leasing corporation was incorporated in 1952. With the passage of time, particularly during the early sixties the concept of leasing developed widely not only in advanced countries such as U. S. A., Japan, U. K., and West Germany but also developed in developing countries such as Malaysia, Korea, Brazil and Philippines etc. It has been observed in a study done by a well known International Journal '*FORTUNE*' that the leasing got tremendous success in USA. In USA leasing has become biggest external source of equipment finance. It is bigger than bonds, bigger than stock, bigger than commercial mortgage and is the fastest growing too in the country.

In India, too the concept began in the seventies but the early eighties saw an unprecedented interest and suddenly a large number of entrepreneurs, both new and established the fray of leasing. In India, the implementation of Chore Committee recommendations posed the problem of resource crisis before the term lending institutions. This situation forced the private corporate sector to evolve alternative source of finance and in the situation, option of leasing their capital equipment emerged as best suited to their requirement. The concept of leasing has acquired momentum in India in a very short time. In India, a number of public and private companies offered lease finance at attractive terms.

Lease Evaluation

Evaluation of lease option presupposes that an investment proposal has already been appraised and found to be profitable both under buy option and lease option. It is only thereafter that the question of choosing between buy option and lease option becomes operationally significant.

While the mathematics of comparative evaluation of lease v/s buy option based on discounted cash flow technique is somewhat complex, its logic is rather simple. For the lessee, the choice is determined by comparing the present value of net equipment cost defined as price of equipment less tax benefit on depreciation under the buy option, on the one hand and on the other hand cost of lease measured by present value of post-tax lease rent paid over a period of time. If the cost of lease is lower than the net cost of equipment, lease is profitable to the lessee. For the lessor, it is again comparison of net cost of equipment defined as above, on the one hand and income from lease measured by present value of flow of post-tax lease rent received. If income from lease is higher than net cost of equipment, lease is profitable to lessor also.

It may be emphasised that the outcome of evaluation exercise for lessee and lessor depends crucially on four basic parameters—

(i) Discount rates of both lessor and lessee;

(ii) Tax paying position factor a lessor and a lessee are subject;

(iii) Tax paying position of both and;

(iv) The critical timing factor implicit in the schedule of lease rent.

Evaluation Models

Five different models will bring out the crucial role played by the above parameters.

Model No 1

This is based on the assumption that the three basic parameters (first three) are the same for both lessor and lessee. The other assumptions relate to numbers. These are (i) Capital cost of equipment Rs. 1000\-; (ii) Annual lease rent to be paid in advance in every year Rs. 240/-; (iii)Primary term of lease 5 years; (iv) 100%

initial depreciation allowance; (v) Effective tax rate 50%; (vi) Pre-tax discount rate 14% (post tax 7%) and (vii) funding out of borrowing only.

On this basis, NV for the lessor is Rs. 26.8. The lease structure is profitable to him. However, for the lessee, there is net loss on leasing amounting to Rs. 26/-. Thus the lease deal will not go through. Leasing would be beneficial to a lessee if one or more of the three conditions are fulfilled, First, discount rate for a lessee is adequately higher than that for the lessor. Second, effective tax rate for a lessee is lower than that for a lessor. Third, a lessee is in a no tax position either during the entire lease term or for some initial years, while a lessor is in a tax paying position. This assumption about the lessor is crucial because the determination of lease rent profitable to the lessor depends crucially on his having the tax shelter on depreciation.

Model No. 2

Only one assumption is altered. Higher pre-tax discount rate at 22% is assumed for the lessee. Vee for the lessee works out to be positive at Rs. 8/-. this model is not unrealistic. The discount rate for lessee could be higher for various reasons. A lessor's credit worthiness may be better than that of a lessee resulting in lower cost of borrowing for a lessor. The degree of risk of risk for a lessor could be comparatively lower than that for a lessee because a lessor is able to spread the risk among many companies. Further, debt-equity ratio of a lessor is normally much higher than that of a lessee implying lower weighted average cost of funds for the lessor.

Model 3

Differing tax rates for lessor and lessee could also convert an unprofitable lease structure of Model 1 into a profitable one for the lessee. A lower tax rate for the lessee reduces tax shelter on depreciation and thereby increase net equipment cost. On the other hand, post-tax outflow of lease rent and post-tax discount rate also increase. The present value of cost of lease becomes higher with lower tax rate for the lessee. However, the increase in net equipment cost, is proportionately more than the increase in the cost of a lease deal when tax rate is reduced. That is why lease deal may become profitable with lower tax rate for the lessee. If we assume a tax rate of 25 per cent. Nvee for lessor works out to be positive at Rs. 6.

Model 4: Permanent No Tax Position of Lessee

All the assumptions of model 1 are constant except the tax position of lessee. It is assumed that the lessee is in a no tax position for a long period exceeding the lease term. This assumption implies that the cost of equipment to the lessee increases to the extent of the loss of tax benefit on depreciation of equipment which was available under earlier model. On the other hand, the lessee also losses tax shelter on lease payments and the discount rate relevant for estimating present value becomes the pre-tax discount rate. The net result is that the increase in equipment cost exceeds the increase in present value of lease payments. The lease becomes attractive to the lessee.

Model 5: Temporary No Tax Position of Lessee

The only assumption different from those of Model is that a lessee has no tax liability for the first two years. The calculation of NVee for the lessee is come what complicated for various reasons. A lessee will carry forward to the third year foregone tax benefits on lease rent during the first two years. The present value of tax benefit on depreciation available in the third year would be lower than in Models and 3. When it could be aimed in the first year itself. There is also similar but little complicated consideration of interest charge. The present value of tax shelter on both depreciation and interest available in the third year reduces the equipment cost for lessee. Finally, pre-tax discount would be relevant for first three years and post-tax discount rate for the last two years.

This model is basically similar to model 4. The net effect of temporary no tax position during the initial years of the lease term is to reduce NVee for the lessee as compared with the model of permanent no tax position. However, it is still positive to the lessee.

Tax dimension and timing factor emerge as the most important parameters in determining a lease structure. These two factors are inter-related in the sense that lease rent schedule (back and ballooning or front end ballooning) should be so devised over the lease term as to maximise tax shelter on depreciation and lease rent. Indeed various combinations of the four basic parameters make the task of formulating an optimum lease schedule a very challenging one. The net value of lessee would be negative at Rs. 61 in Model 4 and Rs. 18 in Model 5 for the lessor in a no tax position.

In a situation of no tax paying position, cash accruals of lessor are less in the initial years that what they would be under tax paying position. With smaller amount of cash accruals, a lessor is not in a position to make large early repayments of funds borrowed for financing the leased assets and there by reduce his interest cost. The cumulative effect of smaller initial cash accruals is quite adverse on the lessor's profitability of each lease transaction.

Accounting Perspective

The accounting for leasing transaction has been challenging task for accountants for many reasons. Leasing as a new mode of financing in acquiring the services of different fixed assets like plant and equipment, furniture etc., has grown in popularity and complexity as a result of capital shortages and income-tax considerations. Lease financing being relatively new to India, the accounting treatment and presentation of leasing transactions has not yet crystalised.

Prior to 1964 practically there were no set guidelines regarding accounting for leasing even in developed countries like USA, UK etc. However, in USA, since 1964, the accounting profession has just asked the disclosure of information relating to leases either in financial statements or in foot notes to the statements. But the guidelines issued by FASB in this regard have been inconsistently applied. As a result of this lease financing has been considered to be 'Off-balance sheet' financing of various fixed assets. This is said to be the main reason for the phenomenal growth of leasing business worldwide and particularly in India.

Under the off-balance sheet method of accounting treatment of leasing, it provides an attractive benefit to the lessees. This benefit arises from non-capitalisation of the future commitments to pay lease payments (rentals) and the future service potentials in the balance sheet to be derived from the leased property. As a result, neither the future service potentials nor future commitments to pay lease rentals will be taken into account to determine the ROI or debt-equity ratio (Capital Gearing) respectively. In addition to this it would appear to have less financial risk number when lease financing compared to debt financing and it would show a faster turnover of companies' assets. Though there was no evidence that lease financing has a favourable effect on valuation of the firm, all other things are the same; nevertheless, many a company proceeded on the assumption that 'Off-balance sheet financing was a good thing.

In June, 1973 opinion NO. 31 "Disclosure of lease commitments by lessee" issued by Accounting Principles Board (FASB) suggested that disclosure of the present value of lease commitments (capitalisation of leases) would be helpful in evaluating the lessee's credit capacity and comparing it with that of firms using other means of financing property. Although this opinion did not require the capitalisation of financial lease, it was indicative of the subsequent decision on leasing. Though guidelines were included in the option for the capitalisation of lease but until January 1, 1977 the disclosure of leases in a footnote to the financial statements was all that was required. Most lessees find it advantageous not to capitalise lease payment obligations.

After many years of debate and controversy the Financial Accounting Standards Board (FASB) statement No. 13 came in November, 1976 "Accounting for leases" with an explicit ruling that called for the capitalisation on the balance sheet of certain types of leases. In essence, this statement says that if the lessee acquires essentially all of the economic benefits and risks of the leased property, value of the asset along with the corresponding lease liability must be shown on the balance sheet under the caption "Lease property under capital lease" (Asset side) and "Obligation under capital Lease" (Liabilities side) respectively.

For the purpose of accounting, FASB classifies all leases into capital and operating leases. More specifically, a lease is considered to be capital lease if it meets any of the following four conditions.

1. The lease transfers like to the asset to the lessee by the end of the lease period.

2. The lease contains an option to purchase the asset at a bargain price.

3. The lease period is equal to, or greater than 75 per cent of the estimated economic life of the asset.

4. At the beginning of the lease the present value of the minimum lease payments equal or exceeds the 90% of the fair value of the property to the lessor (minus any investment tax credit realised by the lessor).

However, from the point of view of the lessor a lease can be considered as a capital lease if any of the above conditions of the lessee is met and in addition the following two conditions are satisfied:

1. Collectability of the payments requires from the lease is reasonably predictable.

2. No important uncertainties surround the amount of unreimbursable costs yet to be incurred by the lessor under the lease. Important uncertainties might include commitments by the lessor to protect the lessees from obsolescence of the leased property.

Once any of the first set of 4 conditions are met, the lessee is said to have acquired most of the economic benefits and risks associated with the leased asset, therefore, a capital lease is said to have taken place. On the other hand, if none of the conditions are met it is classified as operating lease and it implies that the lessee has got the right to use the leased asset over a period of time, but that does not give the lessee all of the economic benefits and risks that associated with the asset.

At this juncture, it is also relevant to mention the guidelines issued by International Accounting Standard Committee, UK. (IASC).

According to IASC guidelines again all leases can be classified into two types: One is finance lease, which is normally non-cancellable and similar to that of capital lease (as per FASB classification) and the other one is operating lease. Accounting to IASC, a lease is said to be finance lease if it transfers most of the benefits and risks incident to ownership to the lessee. Normally lease will be treated as finance lease if:

1. Ownership is transferred at the end of the lease period.

2. Lease contains bargain purchase option.

3. Lease is for major part of asset's useful life.

4. Present value of minimum lease payments exceed or atleast substantially equal to fair value of the leased asset.

When substantially all benefits and risks associated with the ownership of the leased asset are not transferred to the lease, then it is treated as an operating lease.

In India currently there are no accounting guidelines or standards for the accounting treatment of leases. As a result the accounting practices of leasing vary among the private sector companies. A time has now come, in view of a large number of companies entering into leasing business, to evolve suitable guidelines for accounting treatment of leases. For this, the entire concept of leasing and accounting need a freshlook not only from the point of view of accounting and also from the view of all concerned-Investors Income-Tax Department etc. In this context, the formation of Accounting Standards Board by the Institute of Chartered Accountants of India in its endeavour to formulate and harmonise accounting practices, can be considered as a welcome feature.

The Accounting Standard Board should now take the responsibility of formulation and release of accounting standards guidelines for leasing as early as possible. The ASB before going to formulate the guidelines it should carefully study:

(i) The policies of Government and Reserve Bank of India towards the promotion of leasing business:

(ii) The trends in capital conditions;

(iii) The growth in lease financing business;

(iv) The interest of various parties concerned like income-tax department, shareholders etc., and

(v) Financial implication from the point of view of institutional as well as individual creditors.

After a careful study of the policies of the Government and RBI, capital market conditions, growth in leasing business and interests of various parties like shareholders, creditors, income-tax department etc., the Accounting Standards Board has to develop a frame-work for accounting for lease financing. The accounting frame work should necessarily take the Indian practices of lease financing into consideration. A typical accounting frame work for lease financial is depicted in Fig–1. It emerges from the figure–1 that the proposed accounting guidelines/standards can broadly be divided into two parts, Part-I and II. These two parts consists of guideline relating to accounting by lessees and lessors respectively. Further, depending upon the type, of lease, the accounting guidelines are to be formulated both in case of lessee and lessors. At this stage it is very much necessary to evolve the classification principles clearly to determine the type of lease involved in a particular situation so as to avoid controversies and confusion in applying the accounting guidelines/standards suggest. The ASB, in this regard has two options before it. One option is to adopt the classification principles evolved by either FASB or IASC in total with some modifications. The other option is formulation of fresh classification principles taking Indian practices into consideration. Once classification principles are formulated it is easier to evolve the guidelines of accounting for leases. To carry on this task, it is desirable on the part of the ASB to constitute an advisory panel consisting of members from the Institute of Chartered Accountants of India, the Institute of Cost and Works Accounts of India, the Institute of Company secretaries of India. nominee (s) of Reserve Bank of India and the Ministry of Finance, Government of India to formulate the guidelines in a more acceptable manner. To make the practice of guidelines mandatory by every concern involved in leasing (as a lessee or lessor) it is also necessary to include one or two nominees for the business community engaged in leasing to represent their interests. The guidelines standards proposed to be evolved should clearly spell out the accounting frame-work for lease in terms of:

(i) Accounting Treatment,

(ii) Presentation in Financial Statements, and

(iii) Applicability of Tax laws including law of sales Tax.

It is also important to take note of the accounting guidelines/ standards issues by the accounting bodies of other countries (FASB of USA; IASC-UK and CICA of Canada) in this regard.

Conclusion

Lease financing being a new mode of financing in India which has been reorganised as an attractive alternative to debt financing and that has evolved only in the last 3 to 4 years. It can also be noted that the Indian financial markets, especially in recent times, are in a state of revolution which is evident by the rapid growth in number of leasing companies of different kinds. The accounting profession in India needs to take not of this revolution because so far no specific accounting guidelines/standards as such have been evolved regarding lease financing in order to make corporate reporting practices more meaningful and objective. Therefore, a time has now come to lay down clear guidelines in respect of accounting methods and presentation thereof to prevent such large issues from the decision of individual companies and that ultimately results in difficulties in application of tax laws and other related regulations. These guidelines are also necessary to check the mushrooming growth of new leasing companies in India. Further such guidelines ensure that the final accounts of individual companies show a true and fair picture of the company and any of the balance sheet financing is also brought to the notice of all concerned. In the absence of these guidelines i.e. under the 'off-balance method' of accounting the Financial statements may not give a valid picture of the company concerned, particularly in case of companies with the large amount of leased assets.

At this juncture, the newly formed Accounting Standards Boards (ASB) should now task the initiative to formulate and release the accounting guidelines/standards as soon as possible in consultation with the company Law Board, Reserve Bank of India and professional bodies like the Institute of Chartered Accountants of India, the Institute of Cost and Works Accountants of India etc. The important point to remember while releasing such guidelines is, the practice of such guidelines/standards should be made mandatory in case of all companies involved in lease financing if necessary by bringing the suitable amendments to existing laws relating to companies and tax laws.

Figure-1

Accounting Frame Work for Lease Financing

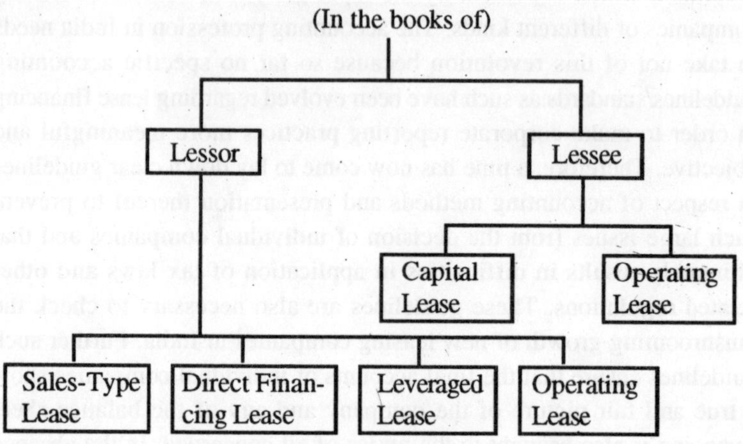

Thus, leasing business is increasingly finding a favourable trend in India in industries as well as in agriculture because of easy availability of finance at low cost; tax advantages; no initial capital outlay; and the facility of "off-the balance sheet" financing. Inspite of these claims of leasing business, it is not free from problems. The leasing companies in India are facing certain problems. They are:

1. Resources constraint,
2. Risk of obsolescence,
3. Non-availability of Sales Tax considerations,
4. Cut-throat competition,
5. Lack of qualified personnel,
6. Delay in return payments,
7. Attitude of the government,

1. Resources Constraint

Lack of licensing requirements from the Reserve Bank of India and the Government was responsible or the entry of a large number of companies into leasing business. As a result of cut-throat competition a considerable fall in the rental was experienced by the leasing companies. For promoting their success of public issue a large number of leasing companies resorted to too much of advertising with a net result that they are left with only 60 to 70% of the capital. consequently, their profitability had bounced back. They failed to earn to the expectation of the shareholders. In this context, it is also important to note that the leasing companies are now leasing at rates that do not cover their costs. It has ultimately an adverse impact on the leasing companies with regard to raising further capital in the capital market. Since the leasing investment involve huge capital outlay, they are finding it very difficult to finance them out to their own funds. As last resort, they have to approach the commercial banks which may charge a very high rate of interest. As a result, the lease rentals have to be quite high, and with that the operations of the leasing companies may come to a stands till due to paucity of funds.

2. Risk of Obsolescence

The modern techno-dynamic age has given chance for obsolescence at a high rate due to technological improvements in production of machinery and process. It will be beneficial for the lessee to have equipment on operating lease where the risk of obsolescence is borne by the leasing company. At the same time the leasing company will get much trouble since it has to bear the capital loss in case of obsolescence.

3. Non-availability of Sales-tax Considerations

The implications of Sales Tax on lease rentals make leasing correspondingly more expensive as the cost of the equipment required under leasing becomes inflated to the extent of sales tax paid by the leasing companies. Further, leasing firms are not allowed to use 'C' forms for purchase of assets which would entitle them to lower rates of sales tax at 4 per cent on purchase of assets, which is usually allowed to a buyer on a loan scheme. A combination of higher rate of sales tax on the acquisition of capital equipment and tax on lease rental payments will make the leasing transactions totally uneconomical. Thus, leasing has become a more expensive from of financing than the hire-purchase method. This tax would add to the cost of leasing in the long-run and is detrimental to the growth of leasing industry and as a consequence to the development of the industrial sector. Perhaps, the ultimate sufferer is the lessee and the leasing business as a whole is indirectly affected on this account.

4. Cut-throat Competition

Though it is true that leasing companies in the West are highly successful, at lease the immediate future of leasing business in India is bleak on account of dozens of them having entered in field almost at the same time. It leads to cut-throat competition and in the process lease rentals have come down to most uneconomic levels. A buoyant market did not exist for all these companies in the segments they wished to operate. Today, in our country, there are about 600 small and big companies doing leasing business. Most of them come out with maiden dividends as promised. As per the report of the Business India, the rate of interest works out to 13-14 per cent per annum which is very much lower than the average cost of capital, whereas they are paying more than 189 per cent in the form of interest on loans taken from the financial institutions or commercial banks. In such a situation, the lease rentals have to be increased. But, it is not easy to raise the rental payment because the customers are used to lower rates and it is not an easy task at a later date to get orders with higher rentals. Ultimately, these companies find it very difficult to find them out of their own capital. Thus, the lack of finance has become one of the important obstacles to leasing companies on the way of progress.

5. Lack of Qualified Personnel

For *entraining* business, success or failure, depends on the quality of the qualified and experienced people. The nature of the leasing and hire-purchase business is nothing but financing the capital equipment. Hence, all procedures like appraisal, judging, integrity and capability of the borrowed party, legal matters, etc., have to be looked after before the finalisation of the matter. Similarly, the recovery of rentals, maintenance of accounts etc., have to follow a special system. Further, the type of these personnel also depends on the training and experience they have gained in the previous job. In India, the concept of leasing business is a recent one and naturally it is very difficult to get the right man to deal with the problems of this new business. Moreover, the small leasing units are not in a position to go in for computer-test-getting by retiring a qualified and experienced EDP managers. These leasing companies are echoosing the retired bank officials for top positions, perhaps on the presumption that they, being in the finance line for quite a long time, can perform the task well. But one should take note of the fact that the modus operandi of working banking system is different from that of leasing business. On account of this fact, operations of the leasing business are bound to suffer.

6. Delay in Rental Payments

In many a case the lessees are not in a position to pay the lease rentals in due time. In the lessor point of view, the late payment of rent has some cost. But the lessor, while fixing the lease rentals at the time of the lease agreement, does not take into consideration the slow or delay in recovery of the rentals experienced later. Further, there is another type of cost involved in the leasing activity which is the problem of bad debts. We can not expect that all payments are promptly recovered, when a large amount is written off as bad debts by the commercial banks every year. Thus, these two types of risks would disturb the future prospects of leasing business.

7. Attitude of the Government

The most unfortunate thing in India is that the Government has never come out with clear cut rules and regulations on any matter. The same is also true in the case of leasing business. For instance, the Government has not so far come out with clear-cut guidelines with regard to sales tax, investment allowances etc.

Over and above the problems discussed, there are many other factors indirectly contributing to the faded picture of leasing business in India such as lack of experienced Chief Executives, meager promoters' investment, ornamental Board of Directors, non-availability of required expertise on the part of lessees to evaluate the implicit cost of leasing insufficient propaganda work by lessors, no feasibility studies, etc.

References

1. Joshi, P. L., *Leasing Comes of Age-Indian Scene,* Amrita Prakashan, Bombay.
2. James C. Van Horne, *Financial Management and Policy*; prentice Hall of India Private Ltd., New Delhi, 1985.
3. Tandon Committee (1975) Report: Study Group of Review the System of Cash Credit, Bombay, Reserve Bank of India.
4. Chore Committee (1980) Report: Working Group to Review the system of Cash Credit, Bombay, Reserve Bank of India.
5. Ghosh, P. K. and Gupta G. S. *Fundamentals of Leasing and Lease Finance:* Vision Book Private Ltd., New Delhi, 1985.
6. Leasing & Financing : A Special Supplement. *The Economic Times,* November 29, 1985, New Delhi.
7. Concept of Leasing: *The Economic Times,* June 18, 1983. New Delhi.
8. Leasing Finance –An Economic Times Survery; *The Economic Times,* November 7,1986.

14

Some Facets of Lease Financing

Rajeev Saxena

The pace of industrial growth achieved in India especially in the recent years has been stupendous. The fact that out of a total Plan outlay of Rs. 3.2 crores in the Seventh Plan, a sum of Rs. 1.68 crores accounting for 53% of the total, has been ear-marked for the private sector investment, bears ample testimony to the increasing emphasis on the private sector for the purpose of economic development. In the early Seventies, the resource mobilisation for the private sector was mainly provided by the plethora of development banking institutions and an insignificant portion was raised from the capital market. The capital market in those days, used to raise about Rs. 100 crores in one year period, with stress and strain. But the same amount is raised today in one issue by a single unit in the corporate sector. Moreover, the number of companies which used to be listed on the Stock Exchanges in India, has gone up from 90 to 900 in a year, thus, recording a phenomenal growth.

Leasing has become a potent tool in the corporate financial management and has slowly replaced the traditional method of equipment financing through term-loans/equity at a faster rate. With the ever-increasing use of leasing by industrial units for the purpose of acquisition of fixed assets, "lease versus buy" decision-making has strongly titled in favour of lease.

Definition

Lease is defined as a special type of transaction where two persons enter into an agreement, where by the owner (the lessor) agrees to provide the full use of assets or equipments for use by the user (the Lessee) over a certain period of time for which the Lessee agrees to pay a consideration (lease rentals) regularly. The International According Standards No. 17 defines lease as "an agreement whereby the lessor conveys to the lessee in return for rent the right to use the asset for an agreed period of time."

Presently, lease accounting is not subject to any specific regulatory code in India, though accounting standards have been put forth by International bodies. In the absence of any specific guidelines to this effect, both lessors and lessees have taken maximum business advantage of the situation.

Of the various types of leasing, the finance lease which is usually extended as a full-payout lease has become popular in the recent years. This form of financing provides the long term use of an asset, in which the "lessor" (leasing company, a financier or lender) renders a financial service by purchasing from a supplier, on the specifications of the "lessee" (user or borrower), plant, equipment or other capital assets, the use of which he grants to the lessee for the major part of its useful life. The lease involves obligatory (absolute and unconditional) rental payments by the lessee to the lessor, sufficient to cover the leasing company's initial outlay, interest and other costs and provide some profit.

As investments are essentially outlays of funds in anticipation of future returns, the Internal Rate of return method - a discounted cash flow technique, is employed for ascertaining the net cashflow as representing the recovery of original investment plus a return on capital invested. Moreover, the investor has to choose from among the various alternatives available, that one which gives a maximum return. In financial parlance one must select that investment in a project which yields Internal Rate of Return (IRR) higher than the cut-off IRR, i.e., the implicit cost of funds used or employed by the lessor for such investment. The lessor can formulate a model to find out the IRR of the lease financing. But the IRR so calculated should be acceptable to the lessor and must cover the basic cost of funds and yield adequate profits. The criteria and the selection of a model may vary from one lessor to another: but ultimately, they will all devolve more or lesson the same set of pre-requisites listed below.

Determinants of IRR

Every lease transaction involves, from the lessor's view-point, out flow of funds comprising the following:

(i) Initial cost incurred in the acquisition of the fixed asset for leasing out:

(ii) Payment of interest at a fixed rate where the lessor has obtained loan from bank or institution:

(iii) Payment of taxes at the stipulated rate on lease rentals treated as income in the Profit and Loss Account.

The inflow of funds emanating from the lease transaction to the lessor comprises the following:

(i) Receipt of lease rentals–direct receipts:

(ii) Tax benefits arising on account of the depreciation on the leased asset and charged to the Profit and Loss Account by the lessor.

For the purpose of calculation of IRR of lease financing, the following ingredients of lease transactions are required:

(a) The terms of loan repayment for calculating the amount and timing of interest:

(b) The terms of lease for ascertaining:

(i) Rentals during the currency of the lease; (ii) lease management fees charged; (iii) treatment of the "Salvage value" while transferring the asset at the expiry of the lease; and (iv) the cost of the asset leased out.

(c) The tax benefits/shelter based on:

(i) Rate of depreciation calculated on the asset leased out;

(ii) Tax rate of lessor.

Once the above parameters are determined, the IRR of the lease-project can be evaluated like any other project. A hypothetical case is illustrated to explain the steps involved in the determination of IRR of the lease project.

Illustration

Determine the IRR of the following lease project:

(a) Lessor has taken a loan of Rs. 1 lakh at 15% interest per annum from a bank, repayable in five annual instalments.

(b) (i) Lease Management fees of 2% of the value of the asset is charged and recovered from the lessee while executing the documents.

(ii) Lease rentals are Rs. 20/1000 per month for seven years.

(iii) The asset is to be transferred to the lessee at the expiry of the lease at 10% of the cost.

(c) (i) The value of the asset leased out is Rs. 1 lakh.

(ii) The tax-rate of the lessor is 50%.

Step–1

Evaluation of Tax Benefits and Net Inflows

Particular	*I Rs.*	*II Rs.*	*III Rs.*	*IV Rs.*	*V Rs.*	*VI Rs.*	*VII Rs.*
1.Rental	24,000	24,000	24,000	24,000	24,000	24,000	24,000
2. Interest	15,000	12,000	9,000	6,000	3,000	—	—
3. Income (1-2)	9,000	12,000	15,000	18,000	21,000	24,000	24,000
4. Depreciation	30,000	21,000	14,700	10,290	7,203	5,042	3,529
5. Net Income (4-3)	-21,000	-9,000	+300	+7,710	+13797	+18958	+20471
6. Tax shelter	-10,500	-4,500	+150	+3,855	+6,899	+9,479	+10263
7. Net cash flow (1+6)	34,500	28,500	23,850	20,145	17,101	14,521	13,764

Step –2

Calculation of IRR of the Lease Project

Year	Net Inflows	Present Value of cash receipts at 15% discount	Present Value of cash receipts at 15% discount
	Rs.	Rs.	Rs.
1	34,500	30,000	29,487
2	28,500	21,550	20,820
3	23,850	15,682	14,891
4	20,145	11,518	10,750
5	17,101	8,502	7,800
6	14,521	6,278	5,661
7	23,764	8,934	7,918
	NPV	1,02,464	97,327

The appropriate discount rate = $15 + \frac{2465}{5137} \times 2 = 16\%$ (app.)

Thus, the IRR of the above lease project is 16% as against the cost of funds of 15%. At this level of "lease-rentals", the lease project is not very attractive since it yields only 1% higher than the cost of raising funds. Any IRR should cover the operating costs and yield profit adequately. Under the circumstances, IRR of 18% would be considered quite fair and reasonable.

Limitations

The above model is not perfect and suffers from the following laxities, Firstly, the lease rentals are collected monthly, but the discounting of cashflows is done on the presumption that the lease rentals are collected annually. Secondly, it is presumed that the lessor is in the tax paying bracket and able to absorb tax-shelters extended on account of the depreciation. This not universally applicable. Thirdly, the transfer of the capital asset at the expiry of the lease period at a price higher than the depreciated value which involves certain tax implications, has been ignored.

Variables Factors

It is clear from the above illustration that there are many factors which have a bearing on the IRR of a lease project. These variables are interest rate on the loan, the lease rental rate, the depreciation rate and the tax applicable to the lessor. Of the above variables, the interest at which the loan is made available and the tax rate applicable to the lessor are not controllable ones. Accordingly, the lease rental rents and the depreciation rate alone are within the control of the lessor.

With the help of the computer system, the impact of changes in one of the variable factors (while other factors remain constant) on the IRR of the lease project, has been analysed independently for each variable i.e., increase in the de[recoatopm rate frp, 20% to 25% and 30%, the increase in the lease rental rates from Rs. 20/1000 p.m. to Rs. 21, Rs. 22, Rs. 23, Rs. 24 and Rs. 25 and increase in the interest rate on the loan from 15% to 16%, 17% and 18%, as represented in the following tables

Table 1

Impact of Changes in the Depreciation Rate of IRR

	Rate of Interest (%)	Lease Rental p.m. Rs.	Deprecia- tion Rate (%)	Discount Rate (%)	NPV of Net Inflows Rs.	IRR (%)
1.	15	20/1000	20	15	96,481	<15
2.	15	20/1000	25	15	99,844	between 15&16
3.	15	20/1000	30	15	1,02,464	between 16&17

It can be observed form the Tabe–1 that when the rate of depreciation (provide under the diminishing value system) remained at 30% (as shown in the illustration), the NPV of the net inflows amounted to Rs. 1,02,464 and the IRR was found to be 16%. When the depreciation rate has been slashed to 25% the NPV has decreased to Rs. 99,844 and the IRR ranged between 15% and 16%. Again, when the depreciation rate is brought down to 20%, the NPV of the net inflows has declined to Rs. 98,481 and the IRR is found to be less than 15%.

It can be inferred for the above that there is a direct relationship between the depreciation rate and the IRR of the lease project. In other words, it would be quite advantageous for the lessor to increase the depreciation rate so that the IRR may be raised, since the deprecations is one of the controllable variable factors among determinants of the IRR.

Table 2

Impact of Changes in the Lease Rental Rate on IRR

	Rate of Interest (%)	Lease Rental p.m. Rs.	Deprecia- tion Rate (%)	Discount Rate (%)	NPV of Net Inflows Rs.	IRR (%)
1.	15	20/1000	20	15	96,481	<15
2.	15	21/1000	20	15	98,977	between 15&16
3.	15	22/1000	20	15	1,01,474	between 16&17
4.	15	23/1000	20	15	1,03,970	between 17&18
5.	15	24/1000	20	15	1,06,466	between 18&19
6.	15	25/1000	20	15	108,963	between 18& 19

Another controllable variable factor among the determinants of IRR of the lease project is the lease rental. When the lease rental is fixed at Rs. 20/100 p.m. (as shown in the illustration) the NPV of the net inflows amounted to Rs. 96,481 and the IRR is found to be less than 155 and 16%. When the lease rental was increased to Rs. 22/1000 p.m. the NPV of the net inflows amounted to Rs. 1,01,474 and the IRR is found to be between 16% and 17%. Similarly, when the lease rental is increased to Rs. 23 and Rs. 24, the IRR is found to be between 17% and 18% in the former case and 18% and 19% in the latter. When the lease rental is increased to Rs. 25 the IRR also remained between 18% and 19% as was before.

It can be observed from the above analysis that for every increase in the lease rental by Rs. 1 p.m. the IRR also moves up by 1%. Thus, a direct relationship between the lease rental and the IRR exists.

Table 3

Impact of Changes in the Interest Rate on IRR

	Rate of Interest (%)	Lease Rental p.m. Rs.	Deprecia- tion Rate (%)	Discount Rate (%)	NPV of Net Inflows Rs.	IRR (%)
1.	15	20/1000	20	15	96,481	<15
2.	16	20/1000	20	15	97,580	<15
3.	17	20/1000	20	15	98,678	between 15&16
4.	18	20/1000	20	15	99,777	between 15&16

It can be observed from the Table-3 that when the interest rate on the funds obtained from bank or financial institution remained at 15% the NPV of the net inflows amounted to Rs. 96,481 and the IRR is found to be less than 15%. When the interest rate is increased to 16%. While other factors remain constant, the NPV of the net inflows increased to Rs. 97,580 and the IRR is found to be less than 15%. Similarly, when the interest rates were raised to 16% and 18%, the IRR is found to be between 15% and 16%.

From the above analysis it is clear that any increase in the interest rate will have only marginal effect on the IRR of the lease project. Moreover, this variable factor is not within the control of the lessor as stated earlier.

Based on the above analysis and interpretations, it can be concluded that a lessor can use the lever of depreciation rate more fully than the lease rental rate for increasing the IRR of the lease project, since the former does not affect the lessee's obligation in any way as the latter does. It is worthwhile for the lessor to go in for funds from banks and financial institutions even at high rates of interest for the purpose of lease financing, as they would have negligible effect on the IRR of the lease project.

Lease Finance: Financing Vs. Borrowing Decison

Leasing is a method of financing whereby the right in the assets leased remains vested in the lessor. The essence of lease transaction is the agreement governing the lease operation. A lease agreement in fact provides for the right given to the purchaser (lessee) to use the asset on rental basis. In a capital lease, directly or indirectly, transfer of property and mode of transfer would take place. In substance, intention of the party is that ownership is transferred to the lessee. Legally transfer of ownership can not take place. Operating lease, on the other hand, is analogical to hire purchase. The Financial Accounting Standard Board (FASB), USA, has stated that a lease that transfers substantially all the benefits and risk of property to the lessee it will be treated as instalment sale or lease sale. It is deemed to transfer substantial benefits to the lessee.

Economic life of the asset and fair market value of the asset have been assigned to a lease. 90% of the fair market value of the asset is transferred to the lessee. Fair market value of the property under lease is stipulated at the time lease agreement is entered upon. The initial purchase price is usually stated in the agreement. Lease term is generally at least 75% of economic life of the asset. Present value of minimum lease payments (MIP) at the time of an agreement is 90 p.c. or more of the fair market value (FMV). Doubt arises as to the reason that at the time of entering into lease agreement how the FMV may be different from present value. Present value may be presumed to be current selling price of the machine. None the less, the definition of fair market value in India has been provided by the Controller of Capital Issues. As a matter of fact, in India we do not have any published information on price quotation. Fair value has been defined by International Accounting Standard (IAS)-17 as Fair value is the amount for which an asset could be exchanged between a knowledgeable, willing buyer and a knowledgeable willing seller in an arm's length transaction. The present value at the inception of the minimum lease payment is greater than or equal to substantially all the fair value of the leased asset net of grants and tax credit to the lessor at that time. Thus lease transaction is a financial deal on borrowal terms and this borrowal again finance the acquisition of asset.

Options

There are two options under acquisition of asset on lease namely: (1) The buyer may become the owner of the asset if he exercises the option of buying it at the end of the lease period. (2) At the end of the lease period the buyer may exercise his option of buying. Period of lease is between 3 to 5 years and may be even less depending on the longevity of the asset. If the buyer exercises the first option, it tantamount to hire purchase of the asset. Instead of interest it will be called lease rental payment. Depreciation will be charged right from the first year on the principal amount exclusive of rent on lease. When the buyer gives the second option, rental charge is debited to Profit and Loss account and no depreciation is claimed on the leased asset so purchased. At the end of the lease period the buyer after having exercised the option, price will be settled as per stipulation in the lease agreement. In the former case it is a financing decision and in the latter one it is a borrowal decision. Lease finance is applicable only in respect of plant, machinery and movable assets.

Leasing is not simple as money lending but it is a development oriented asset-based money lending. The advantages accrue to the buyer (lessee) in that finance is available for acquisition of asset without the necessity of corresponding financial margin; it causes no liquidity constraint to the lessee; as it is off the balance sheet deal the debt-equity ratio of the lessee is not distorted and thereby leaving adequate unencumbered asset for further availment of institutional finance. Hence leasing a financing decision without eroding the liquidity of the business is one year. Apart from that, the benefit of claiming rental as a tax deductible item by lesser adequately offsets the disadvantage of losing depreciation benefits to lessor. The financing might be extended selectively by way of Line of Credit or loans simpliciter or discounting of notes drawn against lease rental. So much so that acquisition of asset is an investment decision, no matter whether it is by borrowal or by lease or any other. Leasing decision thus imbibes both capital budgeting and financial structure. Controversy still persists among the purists as to 'lease or buy' or 'borrow'. Which option should be assigned priority over the others is a matter of financial decision arrived at after having considered all the pros and cons. An instrument of weighing the option has been the ascertainment of the impact of cash flow. Leasing enables a rental package to be dovetailed into the cash flow of a lessee to gain optional tax advantage. During period of high profits lease rentals for asset purchase would reduce tax liability. The companies providing lease finance tender to use interest rates for discounting cash flows, while real cost of capital would surely be higher. Hence a sub-optimal decision might be taken if while discounting relevant cash flows, cost of capitalised instead of interest rate. For any rational purchaser would prefer to low cost-bearing financing mode which will ultimately reduce the overall cost of capital. It is thus an alternative marginal financing decision. Borrowed capital is cheaper so long as interest is deductible from tax liability and cost of borrowing is lower than cost of capital. Purchase of asset with lease financing offers this advantage having lower of cost of debt (K_D) and cost of Capital (K_C).

Operation

As a system of operation, the manufacturing companies are not leasing the assets. The assets machinery etc. are sold or leased by the leasing companies. Hence the lessor and the lessee calculate the cash flow generated from lease deal in order to meet their corresponding obligations to the manufacturers. Net cash flow of rental income has to be ascertained to evaluate the comparative depreciation on leased asset detectable from tax vis-a-vis rental income of the lessor. Present value of cash outflow in respect of rental amount has to be estimated by the lessee and weighted against depreciation. If the rental amount is higher we should not go for acquiring asset on lease.

Lease includes contract for the hire of an asset which contain a provision giving the hirer an option to acquire title to the asset upon the fulfilment of certain conditions. In case the lessee has the option to purchase the asset at a price which is expected to be lower than the fair value at the date of exercising option, the minimum lease payments comprise the minimum rental payable over the lease term and the payment required to exercise this purchase option. Net cash investment in lease is the balance of the cash outflows and inflows in respect of the lease excluding flows relating to insurance, maintenance and similar cost rechargeable to the lessee. The cash out flows comprise of payment made to acquire the asset, tax payment, interest and principal on third party financing. While cash inflows include rental receipt, receipt from residual value, grants, tax credit and other tax saving arising from the lease. The lessor renders three services in that (1) he arranges finance on behalf of lessee which otherwise had to be arranged by the lessee himself (2) he acquires the machinery from the manufacturer and (3) he retains the ownership with him will all risk and reward associated with the holding of title. Even in this situation the lessor had to lease asset with certain constraints namely (1) the Indian tax authority does not allow lessor or lessee to claim investment allowance and benefit of investment, deposit account under Sec. 23 of the Income Tax Act 1961 for assets to be leased out; (2) different state governments are levying and collecting sales tax on the lease transaction. The matter has been accentuated by double sale tax once at the time when the lessor purchases the asset and again on lease rental income. The matter has been aggravated further by the multi point sale taxation in different states. When the manufacturer is in one state, lessor in other state leases the asset to lessee of another state, the asset is used in fourth state and finally the lease agreement may be signed in fifth state. All or several of these states may collect sale tax on the single lease rental depending upon the legislative interpretation. It is thus advisable in the absence of any law that lease agreement should only be executed in that state where leased equipment is to be used. This would waive inter-state confrontation on imposition of sale tax. It is further suggested that the leasing companies may be allowed the use of the 'C' form and confine sale tax payment to one state only. In view of the severe resource constraints of the public sector financial institutions, lease finance may add to the creation of productive machinery and capital assets. This would enhance the structure of capital market in India without going to seek the permission from the controller of capital Issue. It thus play a supplementary role in financial structure of a company by ensuring market for machinery manufacturer. Dr. Rangarajan Committee Report of the R.B.I. has indicated potential for investment in the private sector through leasing business. The only prevailing flaw in that leasing as an "Off the balance sheet transaction" has to be discontinued. For giving a recognition of the finance and accounting information, the amount spent on lease should be reflected either in the fixed asset of the balance sheet or in the report of the Directors. At the same time the liability to pay rentals should be quantified and stated in the liability to pay rentals should be quantified and stated in the liability side of the Balance Sheet. Lease financing is thus in essence, in the word of Donald Gant, "a form of borrowing-perhaps borrowing an asset rather than the funds with which to purchase it, but resulting in obligations which are substantially the same as those incurred in debt-financing." By nature it tentamounts to debt financing and extension of preference for borrowed capital or financing by leverage. The danger point of lease finance is buried in a foot note rather than exhibition as liability in the Balance Sheet. This might complicate the recovery of lease rental when default takes place. The second pitfall of the method lies in that at the end of the lease loses his claim on the residual value of the asset. During the period of price spiral at times the machinery may have more residual value than what was provided at the inception of the lease so much so that the lessee loses substantial ownership benefit. The sale of residual at time may act as a cushion against inflationary erosion of money value. Consequently to remove this ambiguity it is suggested that a standard lease agreement should invariably contain the transfer price of the asset mentioned right at the initial stage. This would reduce the burden of lessor to find a new lessee to take the asset on lease after the expirty of lease period. From the experience it is gathered that the psychological threat of not having the ownership right nor having the stipulation of transfer price of the leased asset inhibit the growth of lease finance in India. Besides this, there has been another captive leasing resorted mostly to avoid taxability known as in-house leasing with the result of siphoning off of profits. Under the Wedlock of inter-company transfer, a group company making large profits lease out machinery, equipment at low rentals to another group company fairing badly, through an intermediately leasing. Likewise, a loss making group company may lease out assets to a profit making group company at high rental through group intermediation. This captive leasing has been an abuse finance and should be prevented from ill effects.

Imported Lease

The separation of use and ownership for financing purpose is the essential condition of a finance lease. In case of lease of imported equipment the following issues are to be reckoned with. Where import of capital assets is financed by foreign currency loans, rupee loans or owner's equity, the user assumes the legal ownership and claims all capital allowance which flowed from ownership. The need for such import has been depended in recent period for expansion, modernisation and technological upgradation. With the emergence of lease, the lessor provides lease finance for acquisition of capital goods. In case the import licence obtained by the importer the same shall be rendered in favour of the lessor. The letters of credit will be opened by the lessor through a bank and the lessor will be deemed as actual importer of goods. All shipping freight and cargo charges shall be paid by the lessor and h will handover a fully-funded leased machinery to the client. Thereafter the lease thus assumes the character of a normal rupee lease. In regard to payment of the asset, the lessor will pay if component of machinery purchased in foreign currency out of foreign currency borrowing or deferred credit, the balance payment of duties and other clearing charges will be made in rupee currency. That is why there will be two stream of rentals one in foreign currency and other in rupee currency. It implies that any exchange rate fluctuation in rental obligation will be borne by the lessee and will be reflected in the term of rentals. Any fluctuation in interest rate owing to linkage with variable interest rate say LIBOR, shall heave to be borne by the lessee. The variation in rental has complicated the matter of claiming depreciation allowance under Sec. 43A of the income Tax Act. This section says that when capital asset is imported from abroad, on deferred payment terms or against a foreign loan, any change in the rate of exchange of currency for settlement of debt, will be added to the original actual cost of the asset for ascertaining depreciation allowance. This in turn would affect the return on lease to the lessor.

New Leasing Companies in India

The new leasing companies which have started operations during the last three to four years are by and large engaged in leasing business only. Most of them do not have source of earning taxable profit out of other activities like banking, long term lending or profitable manufacturing operations. On the other hand, leasing activity on its own ends up in taxable loss in the initial years. A newly set up leasing company is normally able to wipe out accumulated taxable loss in the fourth or fifth year.

This is on account of the simple fact that the proportion of tax depreciation to leased assets is much higher than the proportion of net rental income (after deducting cost of funds) to the leased assets in the first two years. On a rough basis tax depreciation in our country was so far 30 per cent of equipment cost in the first year and currently prevailing annual lease rent is also about 30 per cent of the cost of leased asset for a five year lease term.

However, since the cost of funds is in the range of 14 per cent to 15 per cent for new lessors, depreciation works out to be around double the net lease rent per annual in the first two years or so. Hence there is a taxable loss. Further it can be mathematically demonstrated that accelerating lease business in the initial years does not enable a new leasing company to wipe out accumulated taxable loss within a year or two because there is also simultaneous acceleration of tax depreciation.

In addition, most of the new leasing companies depend on relatively high cost funds such as bank borrowings and public deposits. On the other hand, with severe competition in the leasing industry, the scope for raising lease rent above the market rate is limited.

Inspite of taxable losses one finds that new leasing companies in our country have declared dividend many of them in the first year itself. But this is not a healthy practice. This weakness their financial structure and their long term profitability prospects.

Other Activity of New Leasing Companies

Some of the leasing companies have taken up hire-purchase business partly to have additional sources of income for claiming tax shelter and partly or having high debt-equity ratio of 10:1. Few leasing companies have started sale and lease back activity. Under this, a leasing company buys fixed assets at a revalued price and leased back the revalued assets to the seller company. In the process the manufacturing company which sells its assets improves its liquidity significantly.

The sharp rise in leasing activity in the country has attracted many entrants into the field more to avail of "tax advantages" than help the new financial instrument to reach its full potential. There are to only 'Pure' leasing companies now but also public sector undertakings financial institutions and large industrial corporation adding leasing to their other activities. It is already known that many commercial banks are soon to take up leasing along with their other banking activities.

Most of the new entrants, seem to be eager to "tap" the existing laws which permit the use of leasing to derive tax benefits. One of the ways is to minimise non-lease related taxable income by the use of lease tax credits and the other is the spurious sale and lease back transactions both of which are sure to lead to losses to the Exchequer. The fact is that leasing companies which have no other activities are able t set off depreciation and other tax credits only against their lease income. In the case of others where leasing is only an additional activity, tax credits attendant to leasing are set off fully against total profits of these the financial institutions particularly the nationalised commercial banks may be called upon to participate in a big way in industrial advancement of the country through the provision of the leased assets to the industrial enterprises by establishing their own subsidiaries or by handling the same directly through separate department.

Such public sector leasing will remove the various ills inherent with the private sector leasing and will provide the financial institutions with a lucrative and useful outlet of their huge accumulated funds and the needy industrial enterprises an opportunity to get access to the use of the costly assets without squeezing their meager financial resources in purchasing them. Thus, given the proper direction, the lease financing as a supplement to the debt financing is likely to play a vital role in providing financial respiration to our finance starved fast growing a small-and medium-scale industrial enterprises and financially sick enterprises which are becoming the order of the day.

Leasing Venture of the Public Sector

By virtue of Banking Laws (Amendment) Act, 1983, Commercial banks are permitted to form subsidiaries for the purpose of carrying on the business of leasing. The Commercial Banks are now eligible either to set up subsidiaries with not less than 51% of shareholding or they can invest in the shares of other equipment leasing companies up to 30% of the subscribed capital of the concerned leasing company. However, the total investment in the subsidiaries and share of other leasing companies cannot exceed 10% of the net worth of the bank. It is interesting to note that the State Bank of India Capital

Market Ltd. was formed in August 1986 which is a wholly owned subsidiary of State Bank of India to deal in lease financing and merchant banking.

The National Small Industries Corporation Ltd. announced a leasing scheme in January 1987 for supply of machinery on lease which can be availed of only by the Small Scale Industrial Units registered with the concerned District Industries Centre of the State. This equipment leasing scheme has been formulated to assist the existing, profitable and financially viable SSI Units for procuring industrial equipment for modernisation expansion or diversification of the units. Under NSIC's equipment leasing scheme, a lessee can enjoy the lease benefit initially for five years which can be renewed further on fulfilment of the terms and conditions of lease agreement. During the first five years, the agreement is irrevocable, unless it is terminated by the NSIC for default on the part of lessee.

Of late the IFCI announces to provide finance to leasing and hire-purchase concerns in the corporate and non-corporate sector. The financial assistance will be confined initially to those eligible leasing and hire-purchase concerns with sound financial position which have been in leasing and hire-purchase business for atleast three years and whose debt-equity ratio and debt service coverage ratio are found reasonably satisfactory.

NIC's equipment leasing scheme is a flexible way of acquiring the service of an asset. The lessee can enjoy the benefit of experimenting with the leasehold machinery about the viability of a product/products-mix due to the cancellable clause at the end of five years. But effective lease cost is comparatively higher than cost of borrowing for acquisition of assets. The lessee has to bear annual lease rental @ 24% on the price of the asset (Rs. 20 per thousand). In addition, the lessee has to bear transportation and installation costs, local sales tax on lease price forego tax benefit on depreciation and investment deposit.

Similarly, if the banks and public financial institution channelise the fund available for long term investment to the industry through leasing companies, the effective cost of utilising such fund by the ultimate user (the lessee) tends to rise because of the presence of financing intermediary (the lessor). Unless cost of leasing becomes less than or at least equal to borrowing, leasing cannot be a viable financing mode to the user of asset in the long run. In the context of scarcity of long term fund, leasing emerges as an alternative in the private sector. But it is notable that the hire-purchase and financing business are now being engaged in leasing business which has squeezing effect on capital market. From the point of view of the lessor, if leasing turns up as more profitable than hire-purchase or direct financing business, it is better to switch over to leasing. But this process will restrict the scope of raising borrowed fund from the capital market. Banks and IFCI has decided to diversify their area of operations which may cherish only a costly financing intermediary.

Of late, the business environment in India is undergone an attitudinal change. All sediments of orthodox business practices in all segments of business operations are showing tendency to adapt to wider international business practices.

Lease financing and management buy-outs having been two trendy practice components that are sweeping across the international business scenario. Popularly introduced in America in early 60s and adopted by the nascent high-profile industrial giants like Japan, Korea, Italy, Germany, France etc. in 70s; it caught up with the Indian imagination by beginning 80s.

Indian Odyssey

Abolition of Managing Agency System first and nationalization of commercial banks soon after in sixties plunged the Indian capital market in a quandary. Coupled with a series of controls and credit squeezes, the awfully bureaucratic attitude of the 'nationalised' bankers left the market limpen and jinxed. Business circles started groping in the dark for the alternatives that would fill the void with dependable and interference-free system of financing. Their search was accentuated by the maiden growth buoyancy and some metamorphic changes that were taking place around the world capital market. The Indian scene was bleak. The development agencies like the Industrial Development Bank of India (IDBI), Industrial Finance Corporation of India Ltd. (ICICI) Unit Trust of India (UTI), Life Insurance Corporation of India (LIC); sitting upon the critical productive resource and responsible for canalising industrial finance had developed indifference, ignorance and callousness about growth objective and failed miserably in their task of monitoring any real growth oriented finance to business and industry. Business could somehow adjust to the bigger 'nuisance' cost of capital but found it hard to withstand the unpredictability and eccentricity of the bureaucrats.

This gave birth to proliferation of a number of alternative business ideas based on private finance. The extensive net-work of registered and unregistered chit-fund and saving companies; private Benefit Chit-Funds (BCs), hire-purchase and instalment schemes, that emerged was a reply to the uppish banking practices. For trading communities chit-funds and private BCs have been the path-breaking experience. For industrial operators Leasing has come as the saviour and moral booster.

Basis of the Transaction

Leasing is a financial transaction wherein one party (the Lessor) commits to convey the real estate to another (the Lessee) for the specified period and for some consideration (the rent). It is an executory contract that binds both the parties under obligatory relationship-the Lessor granting the right of use to the Lessee firm or person in return of rent. The lessor retains the title in the asset while allowing the lessee to hold the possession for utilising it. The rent is predetermined and enables the lessor to recover the cost of the asset pulls profit margin during a primary period ranging from three to eight years. Based on this provision of the Indian Contract Act, the lease transactions have been the familiar concept through mining and land lease deals in India. Traditionally, the profit statements and the Balance Sheet show lease-hold property on the asset side, mostly represented by the 'Lease-hold property'.

The International Accounting Standard Committee vide its Standard No. 17 defines and stipulates its treatment as: "an agreement whereby the lessor conveys to the lessee in return for rent the right to use an asset for an agreed period of time" and that "a lease should reflect a finance lease in his Balance Sheet by recording an asset and a liability of amounts equal to fair market value of the leased property at the inception of the lease". This implies that a lease is a finance lease if it transfers substantially all the risks and rewards incident to ownership. Such lease is normally non-cancellable.

What is New?

'Leasing' as we know today, has come as an improvised version of the conventional lease transactions. It is an extended and generalised application of localised practice in mining and publishing sectors of business. It combines the fragmented benefits of leasing, hire-purchase, and instalment systems to substitute the institutional financing. In practice the real-estate base is also expanded to offer almost any type of asset. A wide variety of leasing arrangement is available: equipment leasing, hire-purchase, venture capital: besides the value-added services like port-folio investment, financial service and investment services.

Modus Operand

Leasing operates in two ways: one is financial lease and second is operating lease. Under the financial lease the lessor's investment in the asset is fully amortised. The lessee has to redeem the value-added cost of the leased assets by the expiry of its effective life as stipulated in the lease-deed. The lessor does not share any responsibility with regard to insurance or maintenance etc. The rental stream is so composed as, to include the principal and the interest component. The contract has to terminate with the passage of title to the lessee. Hence, it is non-cancellable or net lease, Under the operating lease all the attendant risk and responsibility lies with the lessor, so does the benefit, The lesser gains through the secondary market disposal of assets where lies the profit in residuary value of the asset. The income and expenditure treatment is on actual basis and the contract is terminated with return of the asset to the lessor. Hence it is called cancellable lease. generally heavy equipment lease are of the former type and light equipments like computers etc. under the latter.

Within these two types of leases, the transactions may be formalised on the basis of either (i) Direct Acquisition of Assets, or (ii) sale and Lease-Back of Assets. The former mode stipulates acquisition of assets by the lessee directly from the manufacturer and under the latter mode a third party which is the leasing company acquires the assets from the supplier and then leases it to the lessee. Normally the short-life assets with relatively smaller written values are formalised under the former and the heavy assets of real-estate nature which are normally canalised through an intricate system of institutions go to the latter.

Fig. 1

The Leasing Process

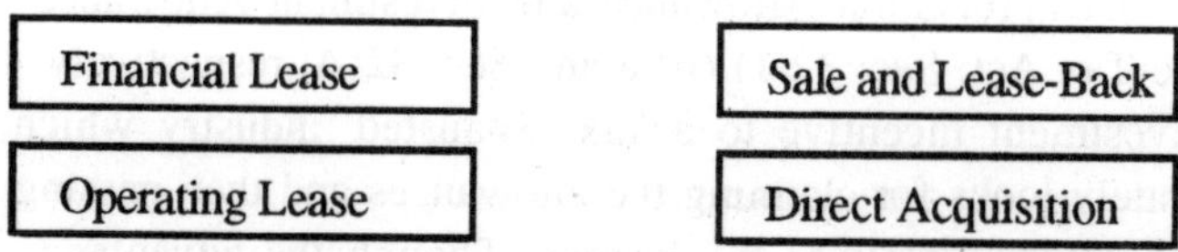

Thus, in a leasing business, a financial institution or an equipment leasing company purchases a piece of asset and hires it to a customer for use in his business. The lessee pays a rent, comprising the principal and the interest to the lessor over the period o use and the rentals are predetermined.

After the stipulated period of lease, the lessee is usually given an option of either keeping the asset at a greatly reduced rental or subject to an agreement between the lessor and the lessee, the asset could be sold, with the proceeds being shared on an agreed basis between the two parties concerned or the lessor may, depending on the residual life span of the asset, rent it out to another customer.

Maiden Interest

Even during 60s some sporadic lease formations are observed which were emulated taking cue from the America's success, but real spurt came in closing years of 70s. No other business idea even caught up so much public imagination as fast as the leasing has done. It is purely for the reason that it is a financial arrangement with ample flexibility. The metamorphosis of the system touches upon three interest groups: Leasing Companies, their investors and the Lessee. The leasing transactions offer some luring benefits to each of them. Its operational simplicity, cost-effectiveness and need-oriented character have charmed all.

L-Coys:

The Leasing Companies have the attraction that its financial business is not covered under the Banking Act, hence no licence, no RBI approval are required. Nor does it attract the limiting provisions of the MRTP Act, nor does it require a letter of intent.

On the other hand numerous benefits are available in the nature of Depreciation Allowance and Investment Allowance under Income Tax Act: Sec: 32(1) (ii) a and Sec. 32-A, respectively. It is a big investment incentive to a 'tax-exhausted' industry which very desperately looks for claiming the allowances and then passing them through lower rentals to the lessees. Though the advantage is not permanent, with a high interest rate of 17.5% the cash flow benefits from deferring tax payments can be substantial. The cash flow savings generated through tax deferrals are generously shared with lessee who probably may translate these inexpensive rentals into lower priced products.

The leasing business has a propensity to generate the high velocity Cash flow, and it has a very low' melting point'. Therefore, a company can start making profit at a very early stage.

The Investor

The investor is beholden to the fast-buck appeal of these companies. No other investment avenue of offers a return of the magnitude of 20-25%.

The Lessees

The non-moving image of the people sitting on the institutional finance works as a sufficient deterrent to many an entrepreneur to plan a venture. A genuinely organised leasing business can offer a wide range of service package under one roof. Relatively it is lower cost funding method where the lessee has the option to retain the assets or return after the use. It is a unique safeguard against the fact growing technology which renders yesterdays, equipments obsolete today. Especially under the recessionary pressure the lessee has a special advantage that he stands to lose a little, excepting for a certain amount of stock and labour. The replacement cost in any case has to be born by lessor.

Above all, its client centred approach as compared to the patronisingly uppis approach of the conventional financial agencies adds a distinguished credit to it. Now the burden is on the leasing companies to look for clients and induce them to avail of the leasing facilities. This financial-marketing has lured the clients all the more.

A Sceptic View

The mushroom growth of so many leasing companies with their surreptitious dealings some times leave many suspecting their bonafides. It is now becoming clear that numerous such companies have been formed with the sole intention to divert a portion of their taxable earning to these leasing companies by way of rental on their equipments and get the same tax-exempted, as these companies are eligible to many allowances. They are working just as another in-house tax shelters from fiscal cover. It is also alleged that they are being used as conduit to canalise the black-money, generated elsewhere.

The zero tax companies have been abolished by the Finance Bill of last year, thereby making all companies liable to pay 30% taxes on their earnings. This has also prompted formation of leasing companies.

Thus more than the genuine 'leasing' orientation, a host of them have been floated as an extended form of subsidiaries, for providing certain cover and ground for national adjustments.

In industrialised countries where Leasing has almost become a catch-word, it is regarded as a highly specialised and sophisticated concept, and practice, whereas in India it is mostly contact-based. Mostly the ex-officials of some multinationals or retired high-ups from banking and insurance line seem to be active in maneoeuvring the credit conduit institutional finance. For them it is no more than 'borrowing to buy'.

Notwithstanding their pronunciation of diversified rang of business, mostly the lease companies seem interested in big ticket or syndicated leasing of equipments.

The 'Low cost funding' base also seems shifting. Equity-Borrowing is reverting to institutional finance with a 2-0-22% mark-up for service charge, ultimately making the capital service show up around 32-35% as the net charge to the lessee. In any case this has to be passed on to the customers.

The companies are also reported to be indicating upon some supply-tie ups with certain group-suppliers of assets with their own terms of maintenance and repairs. This is self defeating and turning it close to the same strangulating practice against the back-drop of which the 'Leasing' phenomenon emerged.

Besides, there are also some malignancy spots at international level. Behind the facade of genuine urgency of leasing, many promoters indulge in unloading their equity obligation as private placing on the stock exchange.

Some try to misuse the import liberalization facility meant for the lessee entrepreneurs. The leasing companies sometimes place order from a optional demand and them protesting that the lessee is no more interested, arrange for a second deal at premium.

Future of Leasing in India

Prospects

The 20th Century Leasing has been one of the three pioneering Leasing Companies in India. It went public in 1982 and became the pace setter. The response and results since then in the entire line has been exhilarating. It is hoped that by the Year-end around 300 companies shall be active in the field, handling the staggering turnover of around Rs. 6,000 crores with the holding of about Rs. 400 crores.

Broadly three types of companies are found in the field.

1. Companies with Standard Leasing operations and desirous of longer-time frame,

2. Companies of dubious intentions. Not genuinely interested in less business but used as conduits for diversification of funds, and

3. Captive units promoted by group of companies for the purpose of acting as buying and selling agency for group/s of companies, earning profit in the profit in the process of doing so.

Obviously, only the first type of company shall be able to stand the test of time. It is indeed to the credit of these companies that the 'idea' has spread so rapidly over numerous aspects of growth and development despite their stated objectives: the leasing companies have succeeded. Therefore, the chances of genuine leasing companies of thrift are bright.

Conceptual Crisis

Nevertheless, Leasing theory is essentially a concomittant of free enterprise, very sensitive to the governmental interference. In Indian conditions, however, the capital market has to operate under a perpetual state of emergency and the omnipotent possibility of government interference at the slightest provocation. A system so deeply ingrained and entrenched is not likely to be changed without a change in the national objectives of planning. Hence the Leasing may perhaps never get entrenched the way it has in other countries.

A lease concept presupposes that its the 'use' of the property that is important and not the 'title'. However, the Indian psyche in a queer manner is almost over-conscious about security and property-right. So that the market attitude and its culture ostensibly appears changing, but can't alter the social attitude The Leasing concept is divested of both the concepts in an overwhelming manner.

Since these two snags are associated with the socio-political system of the country, it has to be seen how they could be removed and the system mended.

Credit Acknowledged

With the State functionaries seriously challenged by the system, perhaps with a quack piece of legislation through the Government, they shall be able to debase or even dismantle it. Yet, it shall lease back an indelible impression on the Indian capital market for ever. It has, along with the Reliance phenomenon and the Peerless Success Story, amply demonstrated that the Indian Capital market is almost on the threshold of maturity, save for institutional finance's debility.

It is in this context that the leasing readers demand for co-operation between the institutional finances and the Leasing companies. This shall free it from the fear of excessive dependence on tax laxity and import-liberalization policy. A synthesis of Government plans and the vigour of this sector shall be able to monitor effectively the health of the industry and also re-arrange and re-shuffle the growing incidence of industrial sickness. The Leasing companies alone shall be in a position to cure the sickness.